Benjamin West Drawings

ISBN 0-911209-36-0

Library of Congress Catalog Card Number
87-60777

This catalogue is funded in part through a grant from
Victorius Fine Prints, a subsidiary of Virginia Metalcrafters, Inc.,
a company working to preserve our colonial heritage.

Exhibitions at the Museum of Art are supported
in part by a grant from the
Commonwealth of Pennsylvania Council on the Arts.

Benjamin West Drawings

from

The Historical Society of Pennsylvania

Stanley Weintraub
and
Randy Ploog

May 31 through September 17, 1987

Museum of Art
Penn State
University Park, Pennsylvania

Acknowledgments

In this the bicentennial year of the signing of the United States Constitution, the Museum of Art is fortunate to be able to present an exhibition of drawings by America's first internationally renowned artist, Benjamin West. It is only through the generosity and cooperation of the Historical Society of Pennsylvania that this exhibition is possible. We owe a debt of gratitude to the Historical Society's Director, Peter J. Parker, and the Board of Trustees for allowing us to exhibit their collection of West drawings. I also want to thank Carolyn Park, Linda Stanley, Anne-Marie T. Schaaf and the entire staff of the Historical Society's Manuscripts Department for their assistance in organizing this exhibition and preparing this catalogue.

Several people at Penn State also contributed to this project. Sanford Sivitz Shaman originally proposed the exhibition. Stanley Weintraub, Evan Pugh Professor of arts and humanities, graciously agreed to write the biographical essay on West in this catalogue. We appreciate his contribution. Arts and Architecture Librarian Jean Smith provided invaluable assistance. Beth Glazier-McDonald, assistant professor of religious studies, and Joseph Cotter, instructor in classics, offered their expertise. Mary Tien and Jean Turgeon volunteered their time and assistance. I am especially grateful to the Museum secretaries, Barbara Weaver and Betsy Warner, for their patience and the extra effort they provided to complete this catalogue.

Finally, I must acknowledge my debt to Helmut von Erffa and Allen Staley for their publication, *The Paintings of Benjamin West.* Without the benefit of this extensive resource and the assistance of Allen Staley, the entries in this catalogue would not have been possible.

RANDY PLOOG
Assistant Curator

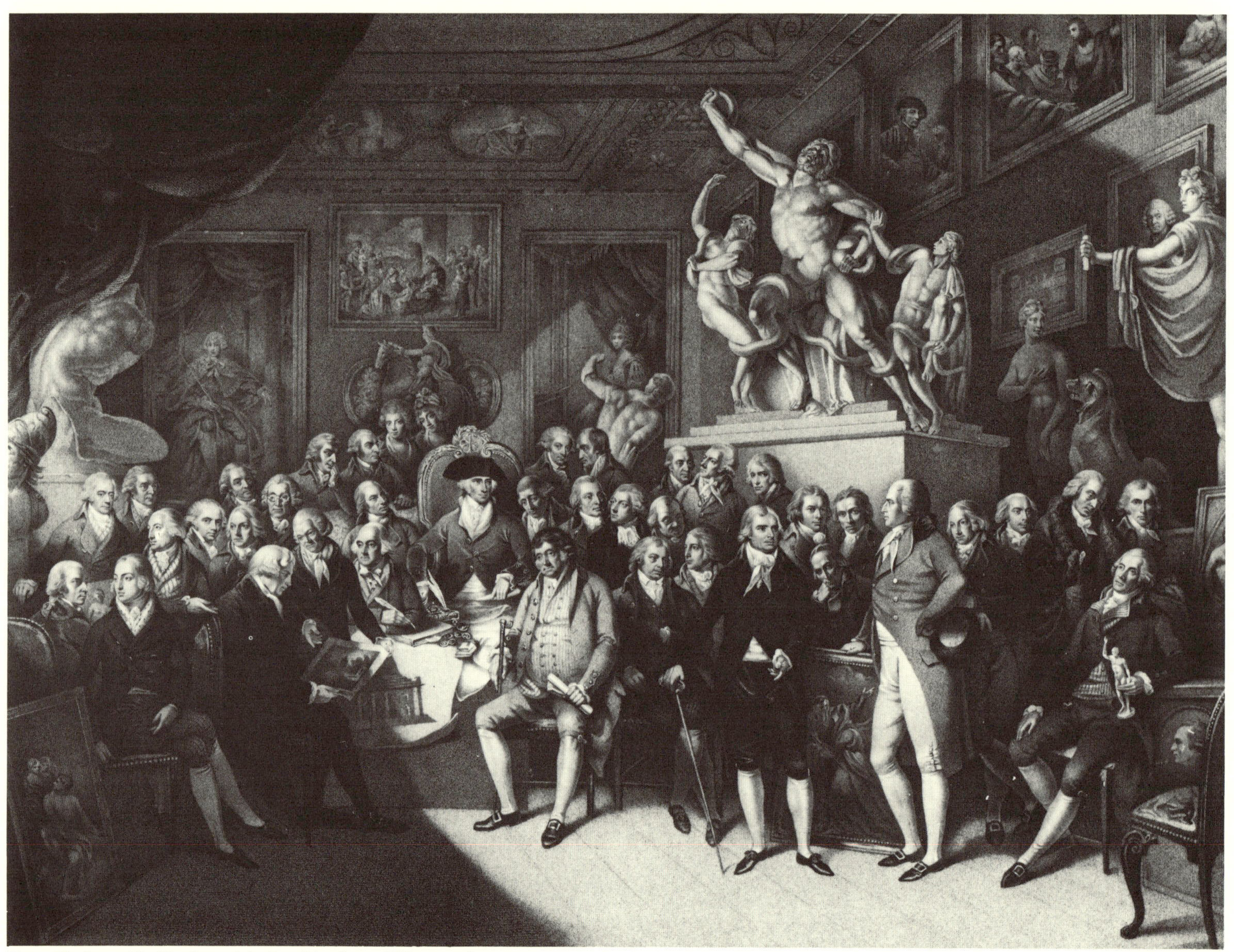

Henry Singleton, *The Members of the Royal Academy,* 1802, engraving

A Pennsylvania Yankee at King George's Court: Benjamin West

A boy from the boondocks whose genius is discovered, finds early fame, marries his childhood sweetheart, becomes rich and famous, Court favorite of the King across the Water, and president of the Royal Academy. The fairy-tale life story was real. There was only one sour note in the saga: He would outlive his considerable reputation.

In May 1802, an engraving by Henry Singleton of members of the Royal Academy was issued in London. Sitting impassively in the president's chair and looking strikingly like George Washington, was a Pennsylvania Yankee—Benjamin West. At sixty-three he was at the pinnacle of his career as a painter. Pictured unrealistically behind him were two women who somehow did not seem seated with the group of men in the foreground—and indeed they were not, as women could not then attend. Yet both were Academicians, one (like West) since the Academy's founding thirty years earlier. She was Angelica Kauffmann, still as beautiful and talented as when Ben West had met her in Rome when both were young. He had drawn her portrait. She had drawn his. But he had ignored the amorous signals: There was a young woman back in Philadelphia.

It had been difficult over the years to keep his loyalties fixed in London. A lifetime away from Pennsylvania, and full of English honors, West had not shifted his affections, but only his perspectives. Speaking of an American painter visiting in 1816, he would say, as if always an Englishman, "How is it that there is more intellect in Americans than in our people?" He was the King's man, but the Yankee pride remained.

Benjamin West was born October 10, 1738, to an innkeeper on the high road to Chadd's Ford, Pennsylvania. It would please his shade to know that another American painter recognized for injecting a special dimension of realism into his art would be identified with Chadd's Ford. It is home to Andrew Wyeth, and its connection to Benjamin West is nearly forgotten.

When Benjamin was nearly five, his father moved to Springfield and opened a tavern on the main road from Philadelphia to Lancaster. The busy traffic of new immigrants west, and of goods to the east, was quickly part of the boy's experience of growing up. But one thing Benjamin would not encounter as a marketable commodity was a picture of any sort. The American colonies were too busy with the basic needs of survival on the largely empty continent to think much about art. Few substantial private collections of paintings existed, other than family portraits carried over from the Old World or painted primitively in the New.

West encouraged stories in later life about his precocity as an artist, and even if no more true than that of George Washington and the cherry tree, they reveal a child who began to draw with his mother's writing pens, and improvised brushes, before he had the opportunity to see professionally accomplished art. Travelers to Philadelphia brought news of the marvelous boy, and sometimes a sample of his art. He claimed later to have learned from nearby Indians how to extract colors from roots and herbs, which may not be *ex post facto* fiction in a country nearly devoid of actual artists' supplies.

According to West, whose recollections to his early biographer, John Galt, make Galt's book almost West's autobiography, a Quaker merchant passing through Newtown Square, where John West had then rented an inn, saw the young West's pictures of birds and flowers, and on returning to Philadelphia sent Benjamin a box of paints and brushes, several canvases, and six engravings—the first professional equipment or pictures the boy had ever seen. They became his school, and the connection with Philadelphia would result in Benjamin's meeting people who wanted a look at the prodigy and his paintings.

A recent settler in Philadelphia, unusual in that he was a painter in a city where the Quaker influence was unresponsive to art, was William Williams. The artist knew West's merchant sponsors, and through them offered to lend the boy two art books—far more important for their illustrations than for the windy and dated theories. The books, West recalled, "were my companions by day, and under my pillow at night." At a cabinetmaker's shop, he procured six scraps of wood on which he drew heads in charcoal, chalk, and ink, and gave them to a local gentlemen interested in his work. The six dollars he was given in exchange was his first income as an artist.

Artistic geniuses were rare in the colonies, and interested parties clustered about West as he grew into his teens. One was the Rev. William Smith, first provost of the College of Philadelphia (later the University of Pennsylvania), who invited the boy to study with him. There West received the rudiments of a classical education, but not much else, as he preferred to paint. In an age when spelling was often idiosyncratic, West could never spell even up to that flexible standard.

His earliest surviving paintings are a fanciful landscape, with realistic cow in the foreground, and two naive portraits, all done when he was thirteen or fourteen. West had little with which to compare his work and only an elementary technical competence. But by his eighteenth year he was producing portraiture of striking character and dignity. George Ross, a young Lancaster attorney, had invited West to paint his family, and his *Mrs. George Ross* of about 1755 is the first stylish picture painted in the American colonies. Success bred success, and by 1758 the Philadelphia poet Francis Hopkinson had published verses in the new *American Magazine and Monthly Chronicle for the American Colonies* that concluded with a paean to the young artist:

> Nor let the muse forget thy name O West,
> Lov'd youth, with virtue as by nature blest!
> If such the radiance of thy *early Morn,*
> What bright effulgence must thy Noon adorn?
> Hail sacred Genius! . . .

Such attention promoted West's aspirations, for which Pennsylvania, and the Colonies in general, had little to offer. Philadelphia at the time was a city of 15,000 and in size second only to London in the Empire, but the domestic market for art was limited, and West's appetite to learn more of the tools of his discipline was powerful. Besides, he wanted to expand his opportunities beyond local patrons of portraiture, as became clear from the gods and angels of his sketchbook at the time, and from a painting he did in Lancaster in 1756. *The Death of Socrates* is a remarkably finished work based upon West's superficial classical reading and an engraving he saw in Charles Rollin's 1738 *Ancient History.* In costume and architecture it had little authenticity, but was prophetic of the neoclassic directions his art would take. It would have been a first-rank picture anywhere at the time, but it never left Lancaster.

Only nineteen, West needed more income than he could get from Pennsylvania commissions if he wanted to realize his dream of studying abroad. He went to New York, where he had been invited to paint portraits, but no work survives of his eleven months there. The venture was a failure. When West returned to Philadelphia, Provost Smith arranged with well-to-do friends to stake him to an Italian sojourn. With fifty of their guineas, he sailed from Philadelphia to Livorno (Leghorn) in April 1760. West was twenty-one.

To repay his benefactors, he was to follow the prevailing practice of making copies of pictures by famous artists, and as the reproductions were produced, more pounds and guineas arrived to keep West learning his trade—for the act of copying was itself an education. His income had to be hoarded for more than survival, for before leaving Philadelphia, he had become engaged to Elizabeth Shewell. West had assured her that he would not tarry abroad more than three years, and accordingly hurried his self-instruction. He studied anatomy, drew (as was not possible at home) from unclothed models, and made drawings for hypothetical pictures he would never paint. As important as his technical studies were his new friends in Venice, Leghorn, and Rome—not so much Italian artists as Englishmen with useful connections in London. One was Richard Dalton, George III's librarian, who, on returning to England, was able to procure for West a commission. Having copied enough historical and anecdotal canvases to have an idea what might be popular, he painted a *Cymon and Iphigenia,* from an episode in the *Decameron.* Simultaneously it fulfilled his assignment from his Italian mentor, Anton Raphael Mengs: "Paint a historical subject to be exhibited to the Roman public."

Fortunately, the Seven Years' War, in which the principals were France and England, had just ended. It became safe for West to travel through France en route to London, his opportunity to see French pictures along the way. By August 1763 he was in London, and on the first of September he wrote to his Philadelphia friend Joseph Shippen, "I am at last arrived at the mother country, which we Americans are all so desirous to see. . . ." The key word, perhaps, was *Americans*—the recognition of an identity different from the mother country. It was not West's intention to remain in England: He had promises to keep in Pennsylvania.

First, he intended to earn what he could through portrait commissions, and to study English painting techniques. Making connections proved easy. He was a young man of simplicity but charm, and as an American could cut through the rigidities of the English class structure. He met a hero of the war in French Canada, General Robert Monckton, who ordered a portrait, and brought West some of his friends as clients. More importantly, he talked to West of the death, on the Plains of Abraham, near Quebec, of his commander, General James Wolfe. In the busy, cold winter of 1763–64, West attracted additional attention on the frozen basin at Kensington Gardens by skating, to appreciative applause, the complex "Philadelphia Salute." Fashionable crowds came to see the young man, variously described in London newspapers as "the American skater" and "the celebrated painter." Philadelphia patron William Allen, in England visiting Thomas Penn, the colony's absentee proprietor, wrote home to Benjamin Chew in January 1764, "My Lady Juliana Penn called upon us to go and see our Country man Wests painting. He is really a wonder of a man and has so far outstripped all the painters of his time as to get into high esteem at once. . . . If he keeps his health he will make money very fast, he is not likely to return among us so that you will not be able to have Mrs. Chew and your little flock painted."

Provost Smith was also in London, and he and Allen weighed with West the pros and cons of returning home to marry and make a living in Pennsylvania. In America he would have no serious rivals, and could be the master portraitist of his time and place. But he had no desire to spend his life painting portraits, especially at likely American prices. As early as his *Socrates,* in Lancaster, he had known what he really wanted, and the Roman canvas from Boccaccio had only reinforced his sense of goals. A trip back to America now would halt the momentum he had generated. By the time he returned—voyages were slow and far from sure on the North Atlantic, and reputations easily lost when not reinforced—he might be forgotten. Instead, his Pennsylvania patrons offered the patient Betsy

Shewell escorts of the utmost respectability to accompany her to London, where she would be immediately married.

In June the future Mrs. West sailed from Philadelphia, under the chaperonage of Benjamin's father, and her own cousin, the painter Matthew Pratt. On September 2, 1764, Betsy and Benjamin were married, and Pratt remained to become West's first American student. Over the years, dozens of aspiring American painters would knock at West's door. West was twenty-four. Pratt was twenty-nine.

West realized that at least for a while he would have to make his living by portraiture, and busied himself painting visiting Americans as well as English gentlemen and their ladies. Even so, his first years in London had already established his credentials as a narrative painter. His 1763 *Cymon and Iphigenia* is now lost, but it had been exhibited in London along with an *Angelica and Medoro,* probably begun in Rome; both were praised. At his new quarters in Castle Street, near Leicester Square, West received the Rev. Dr. William Markham, headmaster of Westminster School, and a friend of Samuel Johnson and Edmund Burke. An admirer of West's work, Markham lauded him to an influential trustee of the school, the Marquess of Rockingham, who offered the young American a continuing engagement at £700 a year, to paint historical pictures for his mansion at Malton in Yorkshire. Rockingham, the future prime minister, was a conduit to other commissions, and possibly to fortune if not fame. West was flattered.

William Allen was still in London, and West sought him out. The Pennsylvania judge warned that the Whig leader was a political opponent to the King, and that if one served a single master, this was the wrong choice. West put temptation aside and settled into matrimony with more prospects than pounds in his pocket. Commissions for portraits kept him going, but his real interest remained the narrative pictures he had studied—and copied—in Italy, largely mythological and classical subjects. The first completed in England, a 1764 *The Choice of Hercules,* owed its inspiration to a canvas by Nicholas Poussin, which West had seen at a country house in Wiltshire, and may reflect his own dilemma in making a choice between simple America and sophisticated England. Several other paintings he would do in the years when he was learning his trade and cultivating patronage emulate other works he saw then in England or recalled from memories or drawings from Italy.

Since West's pictures were illustrated moralities, whether from myth or early history, the Archbishop of York, Robert Hay Drummond, took a fancy to the painter. With West at his table, Drummond preached to his other guests "the honour which the patronage of genius confers upon the rich." To West himself, the Primate of All England read aloud a passage from the *Annals* of Tacitus about the popular Roman general Germanicus, who was ordered murdered by the jealous Emperor Tiberius. Agrippina, the general's wife, had his body cremated, and with her children and her husband's urn, sailed for Brundisium, where his grieving officers met her, raising to a higher pitch her act of defiance to tyranny. Drummond challenged West to dramatize that virtue and courage, and the result was one of West's most inspired paintings, where the draped central figure of family and retainers have a sculptural nobility, possibly derived from the *Ara Pacis* he must have seen in Rome.

Excited by the results, the Archbishop began a campaign to raise £3,000 to free West to paint nothing but exemplary histories. Only managing half what he felt was needed, Drummond went to the young king, George III, and asked him to look at the canvas. West carried it in himself, and with the King went from chamber to chamber in Buckingham House looking for the most advantageous light. (The painting itself is dramatically lighted.) Impressed, George summoned his queen, Charlotte, and told her the story of Agrippina and Germanicus. "There is another noble Roman subject that corresponds to this one," the King suggested to West, "and I believe it also has never been well painted. I mean the final departure of Regulus from Rome. Would it not make a fine picture?"

Whether or not West had ever heard of Regulus, he agreed. "Then," continued the King, "you shall paint it for me." He called for Livy's history of Rome, and proceeded to read to West the story of Regulus's captivity by the Carthaginians, his release on parole, and his advice to Rome not to ransom any of its prisoners, including himself. Then Regulus left Rome to return to certain martyrdom.

The King commanded West to return with a sketch. West posed his American pupil Charles Peale as Regulus, and returned with ideas for a painting. Conducting his new friend to one of his apartments, the King pointed out the space for the picture, seven feet, four inches by ten feet. West was struck by the fact that there were two other empty panels of that size in the room. It focused his mind enormously.

Other commissions followed, and in 1772 West was appointed Historical Painter to the King. For *The Departure of Regulus* he had made more than fifty drawings, and it became his practice to discuss his work with the King—almost his exact contemporary—and to spend some evenings, often late into the night, with his patron, the sketches only a springboard for other discussions. For *Regulus* the King paid £420, and ordered two more pictures for the other panels in the same room. The price sounds modest now for a large canvas, but in today's dollars it means about $40,000.

Whether or not the King liked West's art, he understood that the young American would acquire a great reputation in England. The connection also had other uses for the King. From West he learned of dissension in the venerable Society of Artists, 211 strong, and through West he encouraged a small group to form a new, elite organization of artists, to which he would be patron.

The outcome was the Royal Academy. West was one of the founding members, and, after Sir Joshua Reynolds, its president. With the King backing both the society's and West's own work, his career prospered. Annual exhibitions of the older organization had only begun in 1760. By the spring of 1769 the rival Royal Academy was exhibiting, with 136 works in the first show, including, at the King's instructions, his *Regulus,* as an example of the high-minded art he intended to foster.

From 1768 until 1801, West would paint sixty pictures for the King, many of them featured in the annual Academy shows. His income from George III alone would be £34,187, much of it from an annual stipend of £1,000 that began in 1772. Through the King he even acquired a country house near Windsor Castle, to facilitate his work. Other commissions followed rapidly. Everyone who counted wanted a work by the King's painter.

West knew how well off he was when he received a letter from young John Copley in America, apologizing that he had not been idle, but his time was so taken up with painting portraits (to make his living) that he had no opportunity "to prosecute any work of fancy." West's fancy, meanwhile, was taking a different turn from the neoclassical bas-reliefs that the King wanted, and was willing to pay for. What West wanted was to paint contemporary history with neoclassic nobility, but not in neoclassic milieu. In 1770, the year after *Regulus,* and while he was working on more formal and ancient subjects for the King, West began to paint his version of an already-famous modern death scene.

General James Wolfe, besieging Quebec in 1759 and twice wounded, had died at the moment of victory in the arms of his soldiers. Earlier renditions of the episode included one by George Romney, and another by Edward Penny, with several central figures on a battlefield, in contemporary uniform. Going to accounts of eyewitnesses, West found that Wolfe had died in a tent, attended by two junior officers and a surgeon's assistant. The incident was devoid of size, much like a grand opera without a chorus. Further, there was, allegedly, no heroic nobility in what was known as a "breeches and waistcoat piece." Although painters on the Continent had not always painted histories with classical trappings, Sir Joshua Reynolds and Archbishop Drummond both warned West away from contemporaneity, suggesting urgently that the "classic costume of antiquity" alone would guarantee an allegorical grandeur. Since West's methods involved homework in the histories followed by dozens of preliminary drawings (his first drawing for the *Wolfe* went back to 1765), word of his departure from the neoclassic norm got back to George III, who warned that "it was thought very ridiculous to exhibit heroes in coats, breeches, and cock'd hats."

In the end, the King declined to acquire the finished canvas, in which West treated the event not as it was, not as antiquity might have visualized it, but as it might have happened, complete to an American Indian in the foreground, watching contemplatively how a White brave died. Rather than illustrate the isolated tent of reality, West drew the open plain, with a burning Quebec in the background, and peopled the canvas with a "Who's Who" of military dignitaries as onlookers. The dying Wolfe was at the center, his body in the traditional tableau of a *Lamentation of Christ.* That echo from familiar religious art was to suggest to the viewer the response he was to have, in the way that quotations from classical art had long been utilized.

That West had been experimenting with opposed strategies for handling a heroic death is clear from his two early drawings depicting the death of Wat Tyler, leader, with Jack Straw, of the Peasants' Revolt of 1381, who had been lured into letting his guard down at Smithfield by henchmen of Richard II. It was hardly a study for anything that George III might buy; rather, it shows West aware of incipient revolt at home, and commenting upon it covertly. His drawings often tried out ideas of figure placement, backgrounds and narrative focus, but in the two Wat Tyler sketches, there is a dramatic contrast. In one drawing, in ink and sepia, West drew a classical version of Tyler's death. Helmeted pseudo-Romans, armed with lances and on horseback, fall upon a naked and helpless Wat Tyler. In the other, in graphite and sepia wash, the soldiers are in English dress; King Richard is in appropriate costume for his time; and the surprised Wat Tyler is in peasant garb. When West held them side by side he had all his qualms erased about the most effective and credible way to handle history.

Long after West's death, detractors claimed that he had solicited payments from officers he had depicted to include them in the *Wolfe* scene and ensure their immortality. Perhaps the reason for the suspicion was that he painted replicas for families of two of the men in the picture, a common-enough practice, but using real people was another gesture toward the illusion of authenticity, as had been his sense of actual place and correctness of dress. *The Death of Wolfe* was a tremendous success. Too late for the original, George III also ordered a copy, for which he paid a substantial £400.

New World settings were not new for West. Even in Italy he had painted *A Savage Warrior Taking Leave of His Family* (1760), which was Roman in emotional content while American in setting. While in England he drew two illustrations for a book by his friend, Provost Smith, about a British incursion into Ohio in 1764, and at about the same time he painted a stirring scene from the victory of General William Johnson at Lake George in 1755. The *Wolfe* success added impetus to the American side of his work, as Thomas Penn asked that he depict his father's settlement in Pennsylvania. West's bank account prospered in other ways as well, for he received a royalty from engravings of the picture, which spurred a new interest in reproductions of scenes from contemporary history. West would benefit again and again from the growing market for popularly priced art, and line engraving rather than mezzotint would become the successful medium. The process permitted larger editions, nineteen by twenty-four inches in size.

The next picture of West's to go from canvas to engraving was *William Penn's Treaty with the Indians when he Founded the Province of Pennsylvania,* which had been finished in time for the 1772 Academy show. The exotic setting, and its narrative interest, excited Englishmen, who were unconcerned about the deliberate anachronisms West put in his picture. Again, the illusion of authenticity was what counted. The event had occurred ninety years earlier, but West put his father and half-brother in it, dressed his Quakers in clothes common in his day rather than in Penn's, and put brick houses as yet unbuilt into the background. Yet the scene along the Delaware, beneath a huge elm tree West had played under as a boy, meant more to Pennsylvania colonists because of its familiarity than it would have had if truly authentic, and reproductions blossomed at home on anything which could hold a picture, from china plates to tavern signs.

In August 1772, when West's second son, Benjamin, was born, he was named not for his father but for his godfather, Benjamin Franklin, the most famous of London Yankees. Court painter to George III, the most important American in England but for his fellow Pennsylvanian, Franklin, West was famous and comfortable, and thought no more of impending war between the colonies and England than did his other compatriots in London. With Betsy, Benjamin often met Franklin and other American friends for dinner and discussion of home. Sometimes they would meet on an incoming or outgoing American bark, learning the latest news from the captain, or shipping goods back to Pennsylvania. Never, however, a painting, except for portraits West began in London and finished after his sitters had gone. There was still little American market for history paintings.

Riding his tide of success begun with *Wolfe,* West would do a number of canvases of famous death scenes, classic and contemporary, finally telling Admiral Lord Nelson not long before Trafalgar that he was giving them up because there were no more such subjects to paint. Lord Nelson would provide him with another in 1804. In the meantime he illustrated other episodes, present and past, exemplifying patriotism, self-sacrifice, courage and similar classic virtues; and he busied himself with Biblical subjects for the King, for the Royal Chapel at Windsor and various apartments in the castle, producing dozens of preliminary drawings to try out his ideas. One death tableau took actuality to the limits of taste, *The Death of the Earl of Chatham* (1778) depicting the elder William Pitt dying in a somber alcove of the House of Lords, and exposing, Horace Walpole wrote, Pitt's "crutch and [banded] gouty stockings," which, he thought admiringly, showed the sensitivity of West's feelings as well as a documentation of the causes of Pitt's collapse.

Court painter notwithstanding, West also held court himself—to American artists come abroad to study with him, or utilize his connections and resources. By the early 1770s, West was already known for befriending young American painters, and would do so all his life. Joseph Wharton, of the Philadelphia mercantile family, recalled visiting West in 1776 when a servant announced that a man at the door wanted to speak with him. "I am engaged," snapped West, but then added, "Who is he?" When the servant identified the visitor as a man from America, West invited him in. It proved to be Gilbert Stuart, who had lived precariously in London for nearly a year before summoning the courage—or being impelled by desperation — to knock on West's door.

West's attentions, Stuart later recalled, were "paternal." They were also effective. Gilbert Stuart would be the greatest portraitist of his generation in America. He had hardly settled down when another American appeared, Ralph Earl, from Connecticut, as much a Tory as Stuart had been a patriot. Earl had fled for his life. West taught them both, as he did John Trumbull, who until 1780 had been a colonel in the rebel army, and came bearing an introduction from Franklin, guaranteed to open West's doors. When Trumbull was arrested and clapped in *gaol* for treason, West went to Buckingham House to call on the King, explaining that Trumbull was now a painter and was uninvolved in politics.

The intervention could have caused West trouble, rather than protect his flanks, but after several months, with West and his former student Copley putting up some of the bond money, Trumbull was released and enjoined to leave the country. The war with the Colonies was not yet over.

Living as an American in London during the war had not been easy, even for the Historical Painter to the King. His sympathies had been evident from his prewar associations, and even some of his friends of the later 1770s were dangerous to know, like Patience Wright. Artist and waxwork sculptor, Mrs. Wright ran a pre-Tussaud museum in London and often used West's studio. Possibly an American spy, and unquestionably indiscreet, she also used the introductions for sittings that West arranged for her with the King and Queen to hector them about American independence. West's advice to her family and friends was that "City Patriots"—local sympathizers with the Yankee cause—recommended that any American under suspicion take the oath of allegiance to the King, whatever hypocrisies were involved. They did.

To carry a little water on both shoulders, West painted *The Allegory of Britannia Receiving the American Loyalists,* in which the refugees seeking the homeland's protection include a variety of colonists, even black slaves and Indians. If a covert absurdity was intended, to put his own feelings between the lines, it was masked by West's portraying himself and his wife standing in a corner to the right, under Britannia's shield. He put himself in a number of paintings in which he also did not belong, including *The Institution of the Order of the Garter* (1787), where he and Betsy again appear, less dramatically, a hint that the humble backwoodsman (as he liked to think of himself, especially when he had problems with his spelling) also had respectable origins. Lord De la Warr, one of the earliest knights of the Garter, had been a Thomas West of Buckinghamshire.

Even before the peace was signed, West accepted another American, again with a recommendation from Franklin. Mather Brown, from Boston, because of Franklin, received his instruction "gratis." When Brown's *Portrait of a Gentleman* was exhibited at the Academy show in 1784 he wrote to his aunts in Massachusetts, "I will let them see if an obscure Yankee boy cannot shine as great as any of them." The same year, Trumbull returned, now safely. "Connecticut is not Athens," his father, the governor of the state, had agreed. The art market remained as poor as was artistic schooling in America, and Charles Willson Peale, a former pupil who had returned from military service and was now free to paint, wrote to ask West to try to sell for him a portrait of George Washington, as Peale needed money—but not inflated American paper—and had no buyers. In peace, he thought, the English might be interested.

West confided his "great delight" at the chance to see a portrait "of that greatest of all characters, *George Washington* . . . that phinominy among men." And he asked a favor of Peale—"that you would procure me the drawings or small paintings of the dresses of the American army, from the officers down to the common soldier, . . . and any other characteristic of their armies of camps from which I may form an exact idea, to enable me to form a few pictures of the great events of the American contest."

Peale replied, but West had no idea how hostile the English would be to artistic reminders of their defeat and loss of the Colonies. His first effort was a group portrait, *The Peace Commissioners in 1782,* in which he included Franklin, Adams, Jay, Henry Laurens and William Temple Franklin, grandson of Ben and the commission's secretary. While in London sitting, Adams and his wife, Abigail, were taken, with the King's permission, on a tour of Buckingham House to see George III's West collection. "We gazed at the great original paintings of our immortal countryman . . . with more delight," he wrote in 1813, "than on the very celebrated pieces of Vandyke and Reubens; and with admiration not less than that inspired by the cartoons of Raphael." But British cooperation ended there, as the former commissioners representing the losing side refused to pose for a picture enshrining their defeat. The right side of the canvas remains blank, but for its ground.

West got the message. Only much later, in 1798, did he exhibit a picture related to American independence, a portrait of General Tadeusz Kościuszko, one of the more famous military volunteers from abroad. He abandoned plans for a series on the Revolution, which was not likely to find buyers in Britain, and gave his blessing to Trumbull to take up the subject. More than that, he lent Trumbull his studio in Newman Street, Soho, where Trumbull painted his first two American war scenes, one a Bunker Hill. Leader of the American artistic colony while he painted the King's pictures, West continued to exhibit massive canvases in the Academy annuals, and continued his avuncular way with new Yankee arrivals—William Dunlap, Peale's son Rembrandt, Washington Allston, Thomas Sully, Samuel Morse (who would give up portraiture for telegraphy), Robert Fulton (who turned to steam propulsion for boats), and Charles Robert Leslie.

When Sir Joshua Reynolds died early in 1792, West succeeded him as president of the Royal Academy. The only recognition missing was the knighthood that the office made almost inevitable, but West had declined it earlier, hoping for something better. A son could succeed to a peerage, but not to a knighthood. (As Poet Laureate a century later, Tennyson would hold out, similarly, but with more success.) It was the first of a series of major disappointments that would follow the high tide of acclaim. Next came the clear signs of royal disfavor, as, in the middle 1790s, West became disconcertingly aware that the King was no longer interested in him or his work. Ill with what his advisers and family considered chronic fits of melancholy and madness, George III was actually suffering from the recurrent crises of porphyria, which created similar symptoms as well as serious physical disabilities; and his suspicions of West were aggravated by the opinions of West's adversaries in the art world. Hostility to the Pennsylvania Yankee had grown with his honors.

At court it was alleged that the King's Painter of History, now President of the Royal Academy, was a Jacobin and a democrat. After 1789 and the Bastille, the terms struck horror into Englishmen of birth and title. And West had not only corresponded with the radical Tom Paine, of the notorious pamphlet *The Rights of Man,* bible of two revolutions, but had entertained him at Newman Street and even invited him to Windsor, under the very nose of the King. Even West's compatriot, John Singleton Copley, now more Tory than the Tories, and competing for West's market, spread allegations about West's loyalty and his artistic lapses. West had always managed his dual citizenship with a confident balance, but as his invention slowed, he made the mistake of reworking his old paintings and attempting to show them as new canvases. Copley eventually had one of them refused by the Academy hanging committee as not being an original work. West also had visited France and returned with indiscreet praise for Napoleon, unfortunately at a lucid period for the King, who withdrew his patronage further from West. But he told the painter William Beechey, another talebearer, impatiently, "West is an American, and Copley is an American, and you are an Englishman, and if the devil had you all, I would not enquire after you."

If he were ten years younger, West said, wearily, in 1804, he would return to Philadelphia, and with Trumbull in New York they would "raise the [artistic] spirit as high as it could be." Instead, with no support from the Crown forthcoming in his internecine battles in the Academy, he resigned, late in 1805, from his presidency. While his enemy James Wyatt, an architect, succeeded to the office, and to unhealed divisiveness, West returned to Newman Street and painted his *Death of Nelson,* in the grand style of his *Wolfe* a generation earlier. With no commission for it, he knew he was risking artistic time he might have given to marketable portraiture. He already had warned students at the Academy School, in the bitterness of rejection by Court and Academy, "You must live. You cannot live by historical painting. Do you sigh for riches? Turn the whole bent of your mind—expand all of your anxious and laborious hours in becoming fashionable painters of vacant faces. Are you not equal to this? Then design vignettes for books of travel and novels, or subjects for engravers or calico rollers, or daubings upon china ware."

Although West demonstrated no growth in technique or strategy from his earlier manner, Nelson's death at Trafalgar had given him a subject he knew how to handle. The admiral had died below deck, in the cockpit of the *Victory,* but West, authentic as usual in dress and setting, moved his subject to the busy quarterdeck, with a background of fallen rigging and burning ships. There was no other way "of representing the death of a Hero," he explained, "but by an *epic* representation of it." One had to exhibit the scene "in a way to excite awe and veneration." History was only "a mere matter of fact." West intended "to move the mind."

Massive historical or religious canvases were often created specifically for carnival-like exhibitions, with audiences lured by posters and newspaper advertisements to what was promised to be a grand spectacle rendered respectable by its moral lesson. Back in the raw, bustling United States, Rembrandt Peale and William Dunlap would paint for such audiences, unembarrassed by the dollars their pitchmen took in. When Peale suggested that one of the Master's works would do well on a tour of American locations that way, particularly the allegorical *Death on the Pale Horse,* which might be enlarged for exhibition (West did paint it on a large scale in 1817), West angrily retorted, "I will thank you *never* to name that subject again." But for the first time in thirty-seven years, he did not send a picture to the Academy annual. Instead, opening his own show on the same day, he displayed, for a fee, his *Nelson.* With it was the *Wolfe,* and a similar tableau, *Battle of La Hogue,* both borrowed from the owner, Lord Grosvenor. Thirty thousand people visited, and men, approaching the *Nelson,* reverently removed their hats.

The Queen sent word that she wished to subscribe to the print. West offered to send her the original to examine, and then placed an advertisement in London newspapers announcing that it could not be seen that day in May because it was being viewed by the Queen "by her command." At Buckingham House West met the pitifully ailing George III, blind in one eye and the sight nearly gone in the other — disabilities the King demonstrated to the appalled artist. Royal patronage was indeed over. But West had recouped his fortunes.

West had also propelled himself back into the Academy's presidency. When he was certain that he was exiting as president, he had begun charting a new organization, the British Institution for Promotion of the Fine Arts. The goal was not a rival artists' association, but a national gallery—an institution that would gather and display world-class art, not the annual production of local painters and sculptors. From 125 subscribers among the English elite, none of them (by design) artists, West raised £8,000 and bought a bankrupt gallery at 100 Pall Mall. The new British Gallery, which received the King's assent, stipulated that it would hang no portraits, and charged a shilling admission at its first show in February 1806. West thus became the father of the National Gallery, and by excluding portraiture, foreclosed exhibition by many of his Academy enemies.

Meanwhile, James Wyatt, who had supplanted West at the Academy, had proved a dilatory and incompetent presiding officer. With John Hoppner and Thomas Lawrence each vying to replace him, and the compromise candidate George Dance, another architect (like Wyatt), rather than a painter, the members returned to West, who kept the Academicians waiting for two weeks before he agreed to serve. On January 1, 1807, he was again president of the Royal Academy, and would remain so for the rest of his life.

In the United States he had remained, however distant, a culture hero. In Joel Barlow's *Columbiad* of 1807,

> West with his own great soul the canvass warms,
> Creates, inspires, impassions human forms,
> Spurns critic['s] rules, and seizing safe the heart,
> Breaks down the former frightful bounds of Art; . . .
> He calls to life each patriot, chief or sage,
> Garb'd in the dress and drapery of his age.

Through West's own students, his formula for the historical panorama came to the United States, where it began to prosper long after the appetite for it waned in England. Morse, Leslie, Brown, the younger Peale, and others crossed the ocean with it, and it sometimes created history where none existed, as when Emanuel Leutze depicted Washington crossing the Delaware (1851) in a way it could never have happened, but has since been hallowed by generations of readers of schoolbooks. Even across the Channel, where American artists were regarded with Old World contempt, Jacques-Louis David created tableaux—including a *Death of Socrates* (1787), which owed much to the Yankee from Pennsylvania.

Despite West's pre-*Nelson* squeamishness about charging a fee to view one of his pictures, several years earlier he had agreed to create a picture for just such an exhibition. The Board of Managers of the Pennsylvania Hospital in Philadelphia had written to him in 1800 to request an unsold picture from his studio to exhibit. He had grandly offered instead a painting he had first sketched out in 1794, but had never put on canvas, *Christ Healing the Sick,* based upon Matthew 21: 14–15: "And the blind and lame came to him in the Temple, and he healed them. . . ." His intentions were good, but temptation strained his loyalties to Pennsylvania as the painting, worked upon through the decade, neared completion. The new British Institution—his own creation—wanted it for its beginnings of a national collection. Samuel Morse wrote home, "A sight of that piece is worth a voyage to England of itself." James Rush, son of Revolutionary hero Benjamin Rush, wrote ecstatically about it to his father in Philadelphia. The British Institution offered three thousand guineas (£3,300), the highest price ever paid for a contemporary work up to that time, and expected only a future copy. Since a nine-by-fourteen-foot canvas would have been an effort for a gouty man of seventy-four to copy, West sold them the original.

To Morse he explained lamely that he had new ideas to improve the work: He would paint another, "and give America the better one." It took him most of 1814 to do it, and dozens of additional live models. The painting for Pennsylvania was even larger: ten feet by fifteen. To the hospital he wrote, finally, in 1815, "I think my exertions are more complete in appropriate character, as I have introduced most of the maladies which were healed by our Savior." A further touch of America appeared in the second version of Christ—the hands of Jesus were the first hands that would touch the keys of the telegraph, those of Samuel Morse. Accompanying the picture on the *Electra,* along with a certificate freeing it from export and import taxes by Britain and the United States, so recently again at war, was a letter in which West "bequeaths the said picture to the Hospital in the joint names of himself and his wife, the late Elizabeth West, as their gratuitous offering and as a humble record of their patriotic affection for the State of Pennsylvania, in which they first inhaled the vital air—thus to perpetuate in her native city of Philadelphia the sacred memory of that amiable lady who was his companion in life for fifty years and three months."

The painting was installed in a specially built "Picture House" facing Spruce Street. Over the next twenty-five years, 100,000 Americans paid admission to view the painting, the proceeds defraying the cost of the structure and adding enough to construct a new hospital wing. (In a new setting at the hospital, the painting is still there.) It represented the apogee of the single grand narrative picture as box-office attraction.

As companion pieces, West intended to present the hospital with a full-length self-portrait on a mahogany panel, and a portrait of his greatest American friend in London, Benjamin Franklin. Neither would be finished. The Franklin survives as a thirteen-by-ten-inch oil sketch on paper, of Franklin conducting his lightning-and-key experiment, with an allegorical background and Franklin seemingly in the clouds himself. Despite its preliminary nature, it is one of West's most sensitive portraits, evidence that he had not lost the ability, in his eightieth year, to rise, if only for a moment now, to the best that was left in him.

By then West was painting, largely, imitations of his earlier work, often left-handed, with his gouty right hand wrapped in bandages. Unfashionable now in England, he had already tried, through Robert Fulton, to sell his studio canvases to the new Pennsylvania Academy of the Fine Arts, for a "Westinian Gallery," but the asked-for £15,000 was not to be had. Since he was still Academy president, his decline gave the acerbic Lord Byron opportunity for such lines as

> Meanwhile the flattering feeble dotard West,
> Europe's worst dauber, and poor England's best,
> With palsied hand shall turn each model o'er
> And own himself an infant of fourscore.

In his eighty-second year, he painted his last self-portrait, thirty-two by twenty-five inches—as if in response to allegations of "ten-acre West." Defiantly, he pictured himself still with brush in hand. He died on March 11, 1820, not long after George III. At first the authorities at St. Paul's refused permission for his burial in the churchyard, because his parents had been Quakers and there was no record in England of his baptism. The objections were overruled, and he was interred near Reynolds and Wren. Charles Leslie, one of his former American students, recalled paying a condolence call at West's house, and being asked by an old servant, "Sir, where will they all go now?"

STANLEY WEINTRAUB

SUGGESTED READING ABOUT BENJAMIN WEST

Ann Uhry Abrams, *The Valiant Hero. Benjamin West and Grand-Style History Painting.* Washington, D.C.: Smithsonian Institution Press, 1985.

Robert C. Alberts, *Benjamin West. A Biography.* Boston: Houghton Mifflin, 1978.

Helmut von Erffa and Allen Staley, *The Paintings of Benjamin West.* New Haven: Yale University Press, 1986.

Dorinda Evans, *Benjamin West and His American Students.* Washington, D.C.: Smithsonian Institution Press, 1980.

Benjamin West Drawings from the Historical Society of Pennsylvania

The Historical Society of Pennsylvania's holdings of Benjamin West drawings span the artist's career perhaps better than any other collection. In West's early sketchbook the Historical Society possesses the only large body of West drawings done prior to his leaving America. On the other hand, the drawing of *Christ Bound* (cat. 10) appears to date from 1819, perhaps less than a year before the artist's death.

The American sketchbook consists primarily of figure studies and portrait sketches, none of which were identified by West (see list beginning on page 59). Two subsequent owners, probably a father and son, signed and dated the book, "Robert Enoch Hobart 1779" and "5th April 1820 R. E. Hobart." One of these owners named seven of the subjects: Sammy Worral; Thomson, a barber; Shewel, a brother of Stephen; David James Dove; West (father of Benjamin); John Green (painter); and Francis Hopkinson. David James Dove was an English teacher at the Philadelphia Academy and perhaps taught West. John Green apparently came to Philadelphia from England around 1750 and painted there until around 1785, but very little more is known about him or his work. Stephen and Joseph Shewell were brothers of West's wife, Elizabeth. Francis Hopkinson was a friend of West (see cat. 2). A self-portrait in the sketchbook (fig. 19) is identical to a miniature self-portrait on ivory in the collection of the Yale University Art Gallery (fig. 20). Three sketchbook drawings resemble West's oil portraits of Mary Inglis, Jane Galloway, and Mrs. George (Ann Lawler) Ross (cat. 1). These similarities were first noted by William Sawitzky in his article, "The American Work of Benjamin West," in the October 1938 issue of *The Pennsylvania Magazine of History and Biography.*

The sketchbook drawings record West's early attempts at depicting the human body. They reveal the seventeen- or eighteen-year-old's struggle with facial features, but, considering his very limited training, they also demonstrate an acute talent for observation. Many of the sketches are posed portraits that allowed West to study his subject. Others attempt to capture figures in motion; an ambitious feat for a young untrained artist. Still more amazing are his attempts at the nude, a subject not then available to him in formal studio training.

A second sketchbook contains eighty-one pages of quick drawings, financial records, and notes. The book is signed and dated in the front "Benj West 1790," and the accounts ledgers near the end of the book are dated 1807. The brevity of the sketches makes them almost unintelligible. The single most interesting aspect of the book is a curious list of artists and numbers. It includes Correggio, three; Parmigianino, four; Michelangelo, six and six; Andrea del Sarto, four; Raphael, six; the Venetian school in general, five; Carracci, eight; etc. The significance of the list is unclear, but it at least demonstrates West's interest in the artists it names.

In addition to these two sketchbooks, the Historical Society holds fifty drawings that date from throughout West's European period. Some are signed and dated. Others can be dated with some accuracy by their relationship to dated paintings. Still others can be assigned to certain periods based on stylistic evidence.

Two of the drawings appear to be particularly early and might have been done during West's stay in Italy between 1760 and 1763. The proportions of the figures and the handling of the pen and ink in the *Genre Scene* (cat. 3) are awkward. *Joseph and Potiphar's Wife* (cat. 4) is more accomplished than the genre scene but is not as refined as West's mature work. The figure of Potiphar's wife is borrowed from Gavin Hamilton's painting of *The Oath of Brutus* (fig. 2), which West probably saw in Italy in 1763.

Joseph and Potiphar's Wife is the only example of West's direct borrowing from a contemporary artist. However, many other Historical Society drawings also reveal much about his decision-making process. *The Death of Wat Tyler* (cat. 31) and a drawing of a classical subject (cat. 38), for example, show evidence of West's fascination with the Elgin marbles. Other drawings are revealing when compared to paintings of the same composition, especially when adjustments were made between the drawing and the finished painting.

From the drawing of *The Angel at the Tomb of Christ* (cat. 11) to his painting of the same subject (fig. 5), West maintained the positioning of all the figures, but altered the angel's gesture. The result is a greater sense of motion and increased drama.

In the painting of *Chryseis Returned to Her Father* (see cat. 34), West added an arch, which effectively isolates the warrior Odysseus from the reunited father and daughter.

Agesilaus Rejecting the Magnificence Offered Him by the Egyptian Envoys (cat. 25) was drawn as a companion to *Segestes and his Daughter before Germanicus* (cat. 24). The painting of *Segestes and His Daughter before Germanicus* (fig. 9) is nearly identical to its corresponding drawing. In turn, the painting's companion painting resembles the drawing of *Agesilaus Rejecting the Magnificence Offered Him by the Egyptian Envoys* in many of its details but clearly depicts a different subject, *The King of Armenia and His Family before Cyrus* (fig. 10). Between the completion of the drawings and the execution of the paintings, the subject of *Agesilaus* was replaced by that of *Cyrus,* although many of the compositional elements remained the same.

In the case of *The Death of Wat Tyler* (cat. 29, 30, 31), having no corresponding painting is also quite revealing. Wat Tyler was a fourteenth-century English peasant who led a short-lived rebellion against King Richard II. Three drawings in the Historical Society's collection seem to depict the scene of Tyler's death, but West never painted the subject probably because it would have been politically unpopular.

Numerous other drawings relate to other works of art. *The Demonic Boy* (cat. 9) is a study for a figure group in West's large *Christ Healing the Sick* (fig. 4), painted for the Pennsylvania Hospital in Philadelphia. *Head of Resurrected Christ* (cat. 12) and *Christ Bound* (cat. 10) are both detail studies for larger works; the former for a stained glass window in St. George's Chapel at Windsor Castle and the latter for a painting of *Christ in the Hall of Caiaphas,* which was never executed. The drawings of the Four Evangelists (cat. 15–18) were done in preparation for paintings intended for the ceiling of the Royal Chapel at Windsor.

Most of the Historical Society's drawings are inscribed on the reverse by Benjamin West, Jr. This was probably done in 1839 at the time of a large sale of West's drawings. The title page of the 1839 sale catalogue states, "Mr. Benjamin West, as a voucher for authenticity of his Father's Drawings, has placed his signature at the back of each of them."

The forty drawings in this exhibition are discussed in greater detail in the following catalogue entries. Inscriptions printed at the beginning of entries are reproduced as they appear on the drawing.

Randy Ploog
Assistant Curator

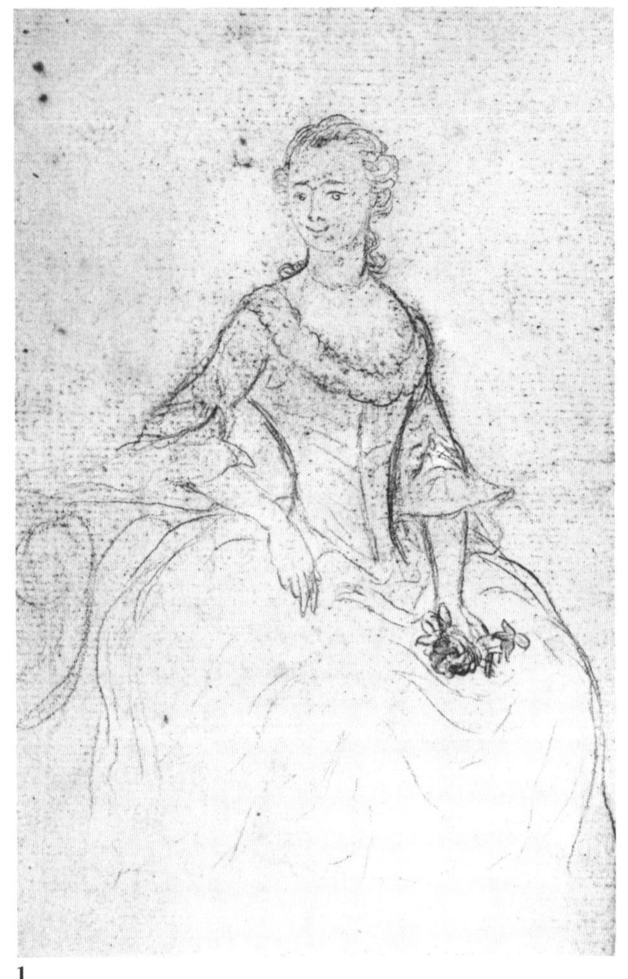

1

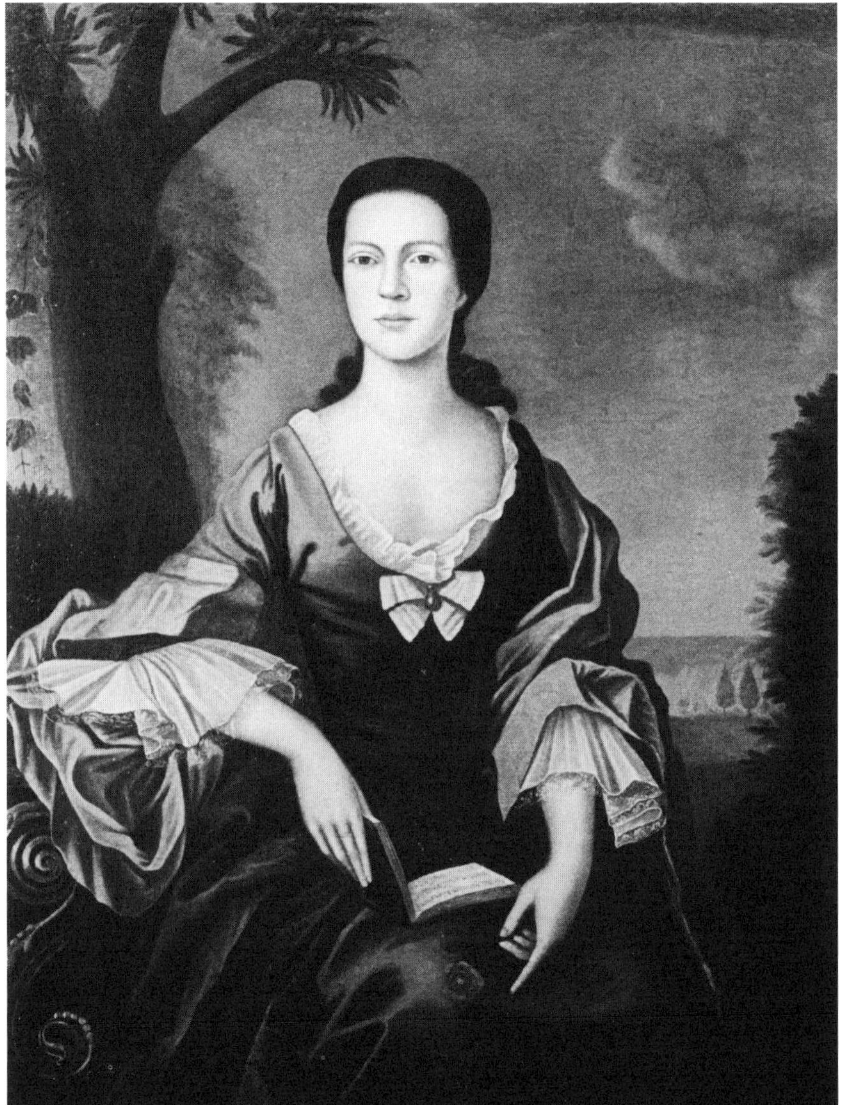

Fig. 1. *Mrs. George Ross,* c.1755–56. North Museum, Franklin and Marshall College, Lancaster, Pennsylvania.

Catalogue

PORTRAITS AND GENRE

1 *Mrs. George (Ann Lawler) Ross*

c. 1755

graphite

6½ x 3⅞

This drawing is typical of numerous portrait sketches included in West's sketchbook in the Historical Society's collection. The subject is not identified, but based on similarities to a portrait at Franklin and Marshall College (fig. 1), it appears to be Mrs. George Ross. The pose, the hairstyle, the position of the hands, the ruffled sleeves, and the inclusion of the flower are all consistent with the painting. Perhaps the most convincing similarity is the scroll-shaped support under the table on which Mrs. Ross rests her arm.[1]

George Ross, an attorney in Lancaster and eventual signer of the Declaration of Independence, commissioned West to paint portraits of him and Mrs. Ross in 1755. West was seventeen, and the Ross portraits were his first professional commissions. West traveled to Lancaster from Newton Square, where his father operated an inn, to paint the portraits. He remained there twelve months, as a result of subsequent portrait commissions.[2]

Considering West's very limited formal training, the portrait of Mrs. Ross is quite good. The drawing, however, reveals some of the difficulties the young artist experienced. The face of the sitter seems to have given him trouble. In the drawing, the facial features are almost cartoonlike, while in the painting the face is cold and expressionless — the least accomplished aspect of the painting.

2 *Francis Hopkinson*

c. 1756

graphite

6½ x 3⅞

West did not identify the subjects of any of his sketchbook drawings; however, a subsequent owner of the book did identify some of them. This well-dressed young man commanding the attention of a woman is listed as Francis Hopkinson. Hopkinson was a multitalented composer, writer, designer, inventor, member of the Continental Congress, and a signer of the Declaration of Independence.[3] He and West met in Philadelphia in 1756 or 1757 through Dr. William Smith, provost of the College of Philadelphia (now the University of Pennsylvania) and became close friends. In February 1758, Hopkinson published a poem praising West's talents in the *American Magazine and Monthly Chronicle for the American Colonies.* The poem "Upon Seeing the Portrait of Miss XX-XX by Mr. West" was signed "Lovelace" but Hopkinson is generally recognized as its author. When West sent for his fiancée, Elizabeth Shewell, in 1764, Hopkinson, along with Benjamin Franklin, assisted her in escaping her brother's protective custody, and escorted her to an awaiting ship bound for England. Two years later, Hopkinson visited the Wests in London and took drawing lessons from West.[4]

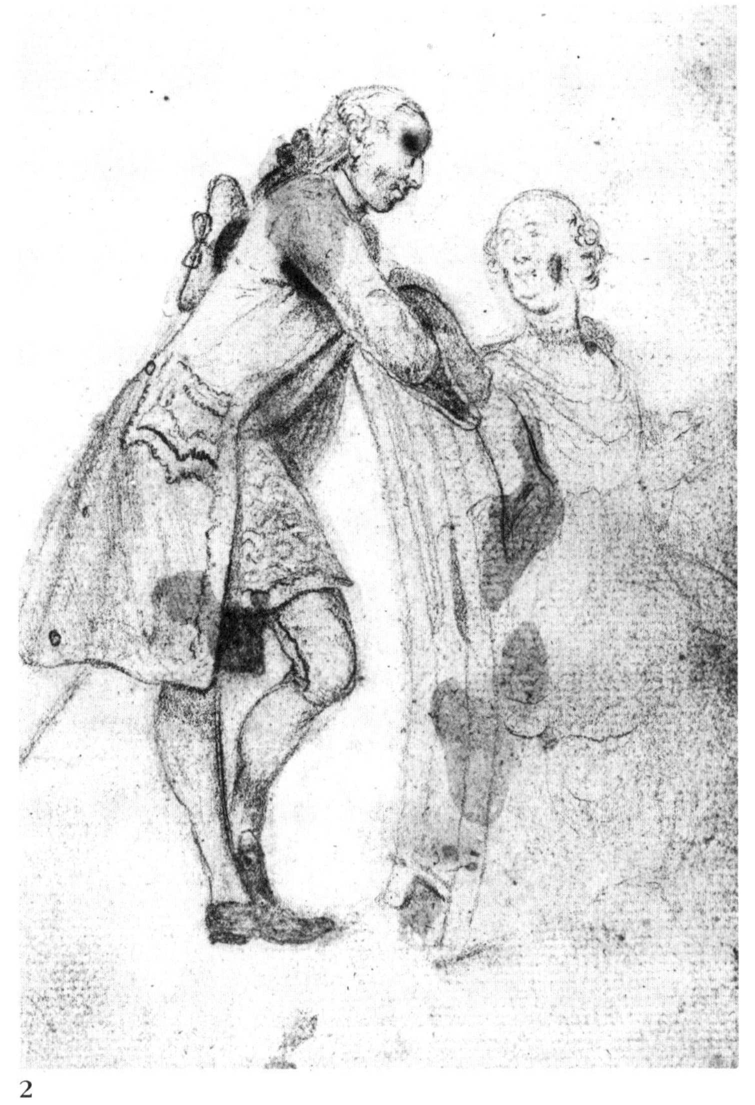
2

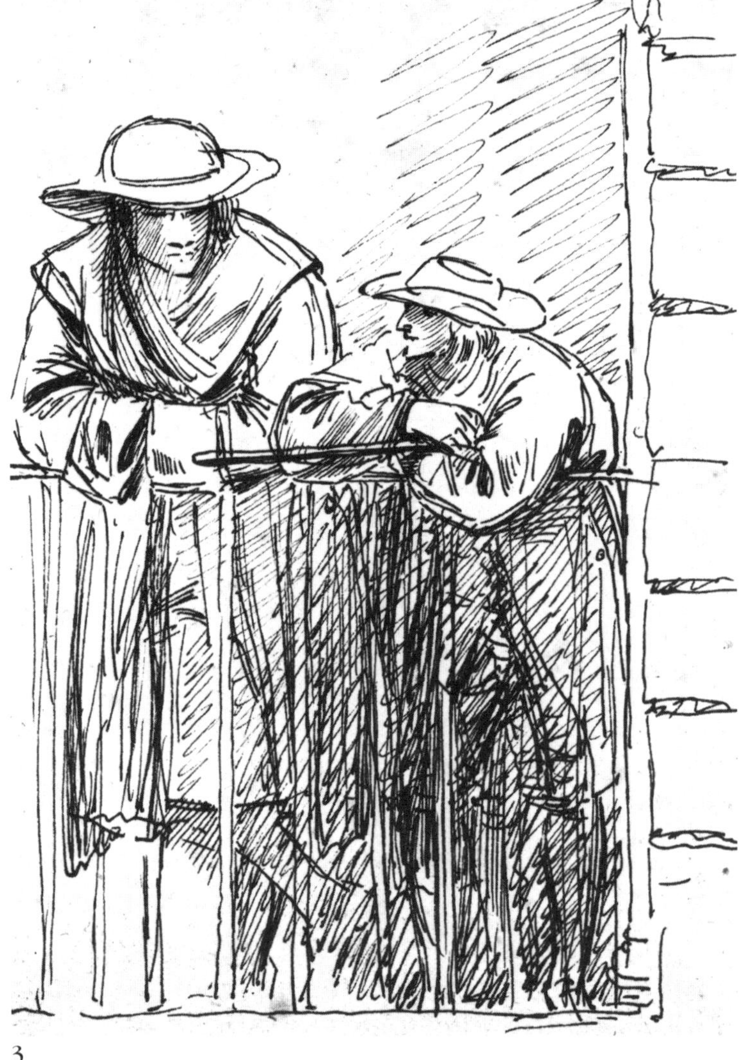
3

3 *Genre Scene*

1760s

ink

7 x 4¾

Inscribed on reverse: Sketch from Nature Benj West

The drawing is probably a sketch of an observed scene, just as its inscription suggests. Stylistically it appears to be quite early, and might have been done during West's stay in Italy between 1760 and 1763. West spent much of that time copying paintings by the old masters, but he also sketched genre scenes and landscapes while in Italy and on his way through France to England. Once in England his attention turned to themes more suited to "high art," such as mythological, historical, and religious subjects. His sketches of genre scenes became rare.

OLD TESTAMENT

4 *Joseph and Potiphar's Wife*

ink

10½ x 7⅝

The subject of this drawing is debated, although, with the inclusion of the pyramid in the background, the setting is clearly meant to be Egypt. Allen Staley suggests *Octavian and Cleopatra* as a possible subject, but adds that Helmut von Erffa believed it to be *Joseph and Potiphar's Wife.*[5] Both of these stories take place in Egypt, but the events depicted in the drawing more closely agree with the story of Joseph.

Joseph, after being sold into slavery by his jealous brothers, became a trusted servant of Potiphar, an officer of the Pharaoh. Potiphar's wife admired Joseph and repeatedly tried to entice him into her bed, but he constantly refused her. According to Genesis

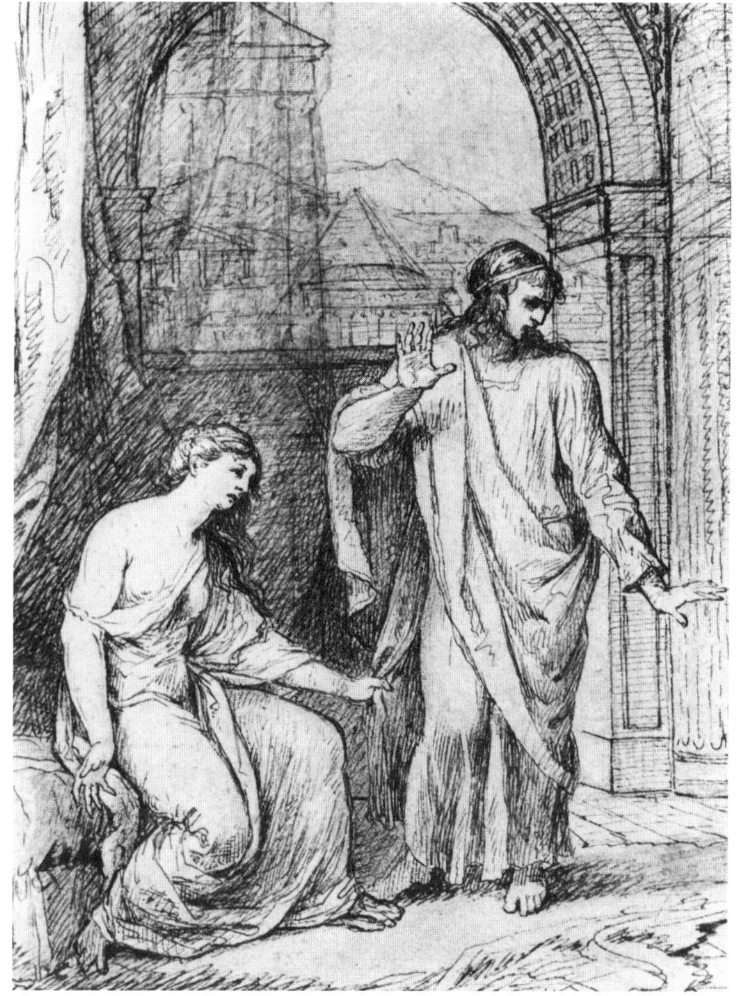

4

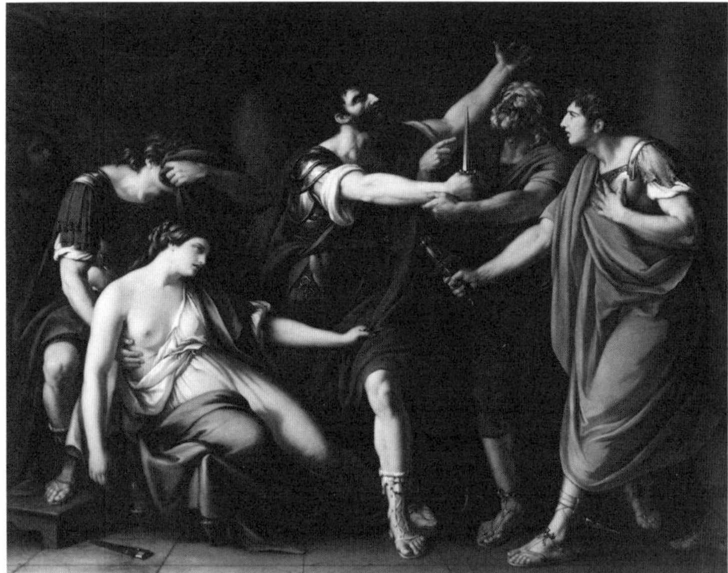

Fig. 2. Gavin Hamilton, *The Oath of Brutus.* Yale Center for British Art, Paul Mellon Collection, New Haven, Connecticut.

39:11–12, one day when they were alone in the house, "she caught him by his garment, saying 'Lie with me.'" Joseph fled, leaving his garment in her hand. Angered by his rejection, she used the garment as false evidence of his advances toward her, and Joseph was imprisoned.

The drawing shows a woman seated on a bed, her hair and clothing loosened. She grasps the mantle of a young man, who raises his hand and and turns away in disgust. It is likely, therefore, that this scene depicts Joseph rejecting Potiphar's wife, and not Octavian consoling Cleopatra after Mark Anthony's death.

The drawing is neither signed nor dated, and von Erffa questioned its attribution to West. Staley believes that if done by West it must be quite early, from before 1766. He bases his contention in part on the drawings borrowing from Gavin Hamilton's *The Oath of Brutus.* The figure of Potiphar's wife in the drawing bears a striking similarity to that of Lucretia in Hamilton's painting (fig. 2). Staley contends that West may have seen the painting in an unfinished state before leaving Rome in 1763.[6]

5 *Pharaoh's Daughter with Infant Moses*

ink, sepia wash and blue wash

5¼ x 8¼

Inscribed on reverse: Pharaoh's Daughter — with Child Moses

This drawing illustrates the story of Moses found by the Pharaoh's daughter as recorded in Exodus 2:1–10. The scene is the daughter's chamber moments after the child's rescue from the Nile. The Pharaoh's daughter attends the child while her maid probably prepares a bed and another servant disposes of the basket in which the child was found.

The drawing is neither signed nor dated. While West painted many other scenes from the life of Moses, no painting of this subject is known.

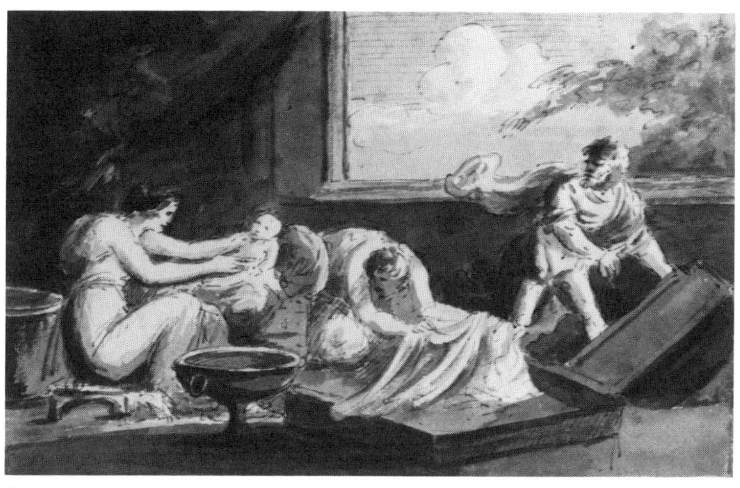

5

6 *King David*

sepia

5⅞ x 4⅝

Inscribed on reverse: King David Benj West

The inscription on the reverse of this drawing identifies the subject as King David. The lyre, one of David's most common attributes, is usually associated with the early events of his life. He is frequently shown as a shepherd boy playing the lyre while tending his sheep or entertaining King Saul as described in I Samuel 16:23 and 18:10. The drawing depicts an older David in an animated pose, but the subject of King David with a lyre cannot be associated with any specific event. Apparently West included the lyre only as an identifying attribute.

The drawing is neither signed nor dated and no painting by West of King David is known.

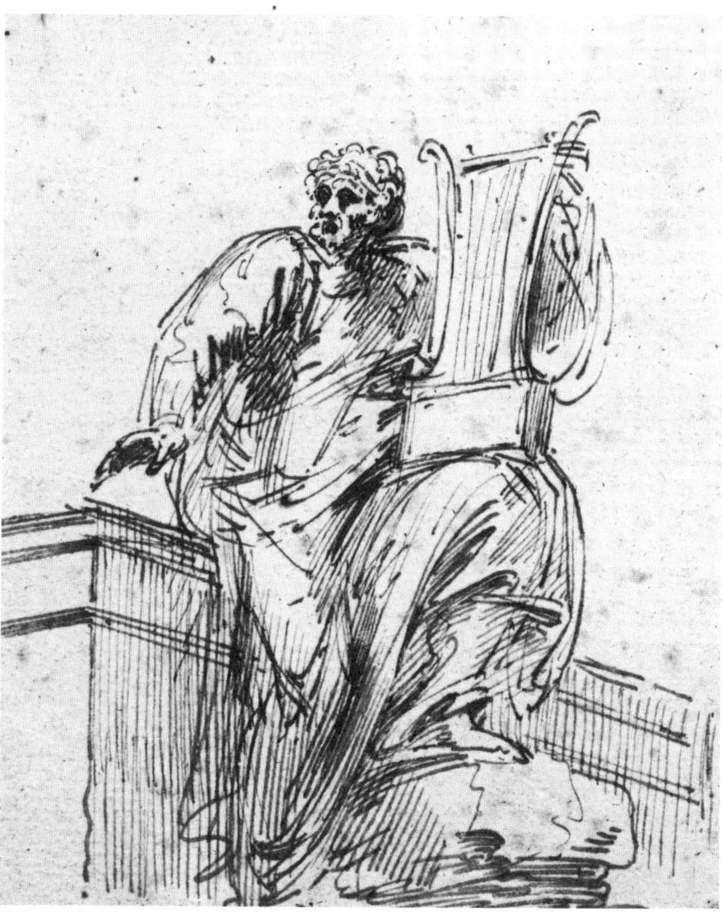

6

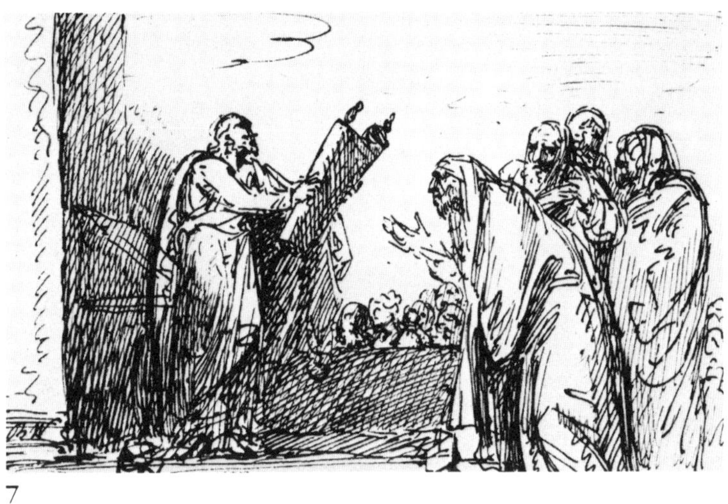

7

7 *Ezra Reading the Law*

ink

3¼ x 4¾

Signed: B. W.

Inscribed on reverse: Benj West

This drawing is signed by West and verified on the reverse by Benjamin West, Jr., but the subject is not identified. It depicts a man reading from a scroll to four elderly men. One of the four humbly leans forward, apparently to ask something of the reader, while the other three stand timidly by. In the background, a larger group of people listens from behind a short wall.

A Biblical event that closely resembles the circumstances depicted in the drawing is the reading of the Law by Ezra to the people of Israel. As described in Ezra 10 and Nehemiah 8, an assembly of Israelites came to Ezra in Jerusalem, repentant for marrying foreign wives. Ezra read to the people from the Law of Moses and formed a covenant with God by swearing the people to an oath. Ezra 10 describes him standing before the house of God, with the people in an open square. Nehemiah 8:4 states that Ezra stood on a wooden platform they had built for him. The man with the scroll in the drawing stands on a low platform with his back to an architectural wall that could represent the Temple. The group of elders approaching the reader might be explained by Ezra 10:9–14, which describes the people as "trembling" with fear and requesting, "Let our officials stand for the whole assembly."

NEW TESTAMENT

8 *Christ Showing a Little Child as the Emblem of Heaven*

1810

ink

7¾ x 6⅛

Signed: B. West 1810

Inscribed on reverse: Christ shewing a little child as the Emblem of Heaven, Design for the picture painted for Hart Davies, Esq. Benj West

The inscription on the reverse of this drawing states that it is the "design for the picture painted for Hart Davies, Esq." The painting by West of this subject previously owned by Hart Davies is now owned by the Trafalgar Gallery, London (fig. 3). The drawing and the painting are identical in composition except for minor details, and both are signed and dated "B. West 1810."

Additional details of the painting's history are known from references to it in the diary of Joseph Farington, a fellow artist and friend of West. On April 6, 1810, Farington wrote that he and Richard Westall visited West and saw the painting "this day finished."[7] He adds that West claimed to have painted the picture in only twenty days, and that

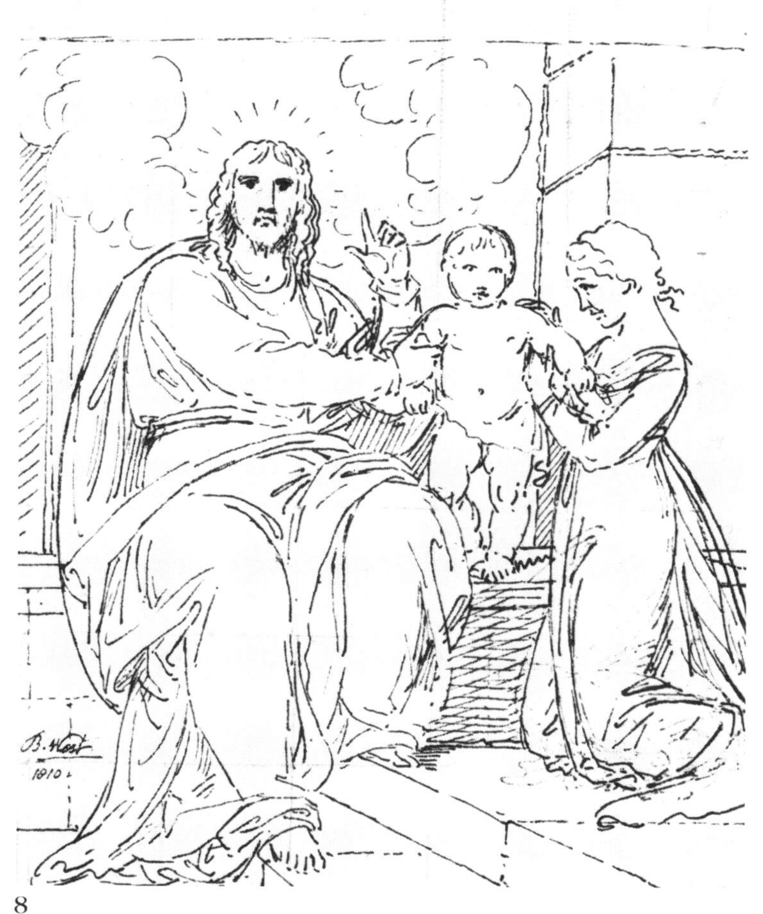

8

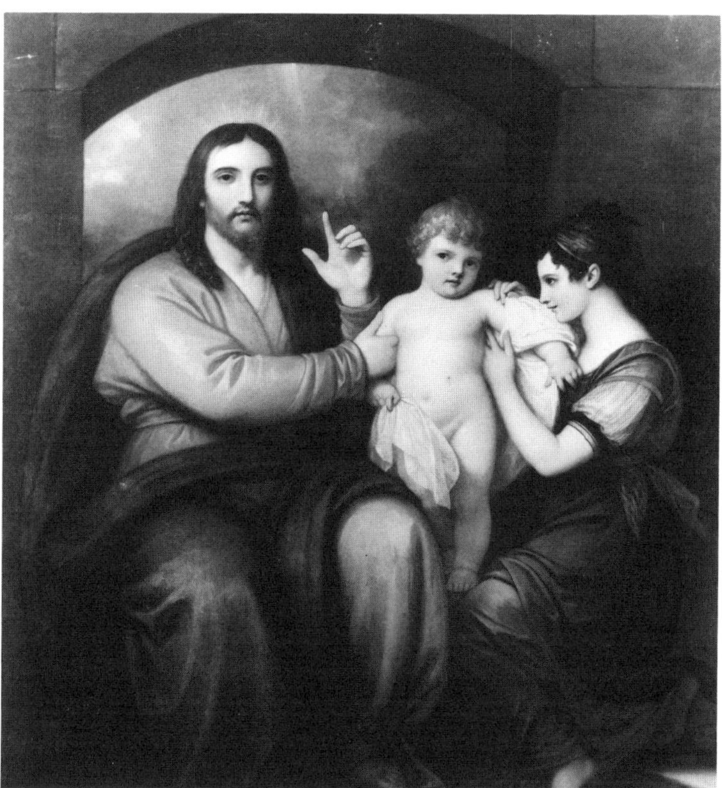

Fig. 3. ***Christ Showing a Little Child as the Emblem of Heaven,*** 1810. Trafalgar Galleries, London, England.

this was possible because his composition was pre-established and even drawn onto another canvas before he began to paint. The Historical Society's compositional study, which is gridded for transfer to canvas, substantiates Farington's statements. The purchase of the painting by Hart Davies is mentioned by Farington in his diary entry for June 26, 1810.[8]

The Bible passage which most closely describes the theme of the drawing is Matthew 18:2–3:

> And calling to him a child he put him in the midst of them, and said, Truly I say to you, unless you turn and become like children, you will never enter the kingdom of heaven.

In the drawing and the painting, a young child stands supported on either side by Christ and a young woman, probably the child's mother. With his free hand, Christ points to heaven.

9 *The Demonic Boy*

1815

ink and wash

6¼ x 5⅞

Signed: B. W. 1815

Inscribed on reverse: A sketch for the Demoniac

Introduced in the Picture of Christ Healing the Sick which

Mr. West presented to the Hospital at Philadelphia Benj West

This sketch of a man and woman holding a "demonic boy" is a study for a group of figures in the right half of West's large painting of *Christ Healing the Sick* in the Pennsylvania Hospital in Philadelphia (fig. 4). West first agreed to do the painting as a gift to the hospital in 1801. However, when the promised painting was finished in 1811, it was sold to the British Institution to establish a national gallery of art. West quickly promised to make an even bigger and better copy of the painting for the hospital. The second painting was finished by June 1815 and left England for Philadelphia in August 1817.

The first painting, now in the Tate Gallery, and the copy that ultimately reached the hospital are very similar in general size and composition. Save for numerous minor details, the only significant difference is the addition of the demonic boy and his attendants to the hospital's version. West felt the addition of this group improved the painting and made it more complete, in accordance with the story of Christ healing the sick in Matthew 21:14–15. He wrote to the hospital:

> . . . I think my exertions are more complete in appropriate character, as I have introduced a demoniac with his attendant relations, by which circumstances is introduced most of the maladies which were healed by Our Saviour.[9]

The Historical Society sketch for this group is dated "1815," the year the hospital's painting was finished. The sketch is not identical to the corresponding group in the painting, but West was clearly considering the existing composition when he made the drawing. The profile of the woman in the sketch copies that of a figure in the first painting, and the head and shoulders of the man supporting the back of the invalid in the foreground of the painting are outlined in the drawing with quick ink-and-wash brush strokes.

Two other drawings of the Demonic Boy are known, one in the Toledo Museum of Art and the other at the Delaware Art Museum.

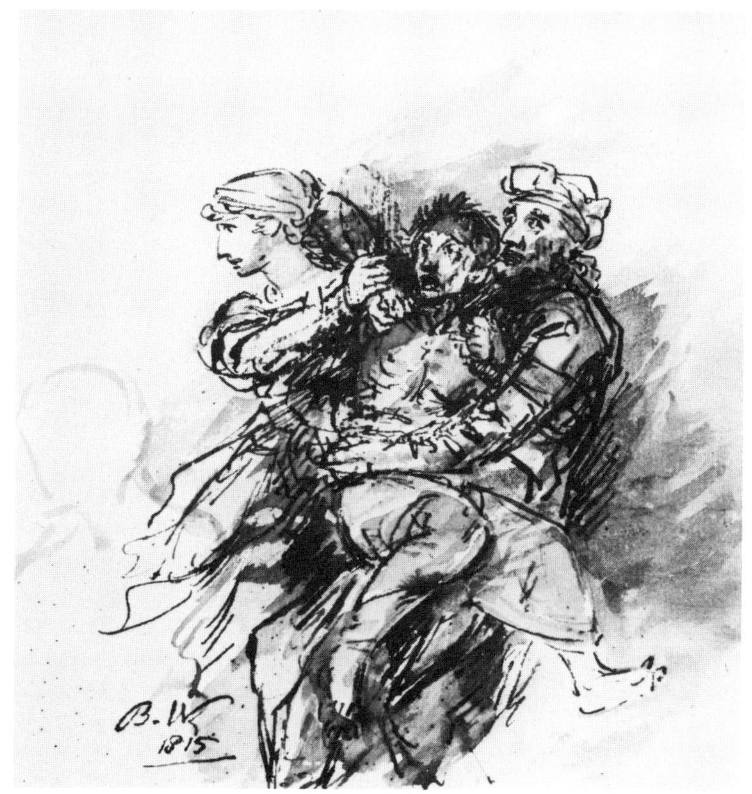

9

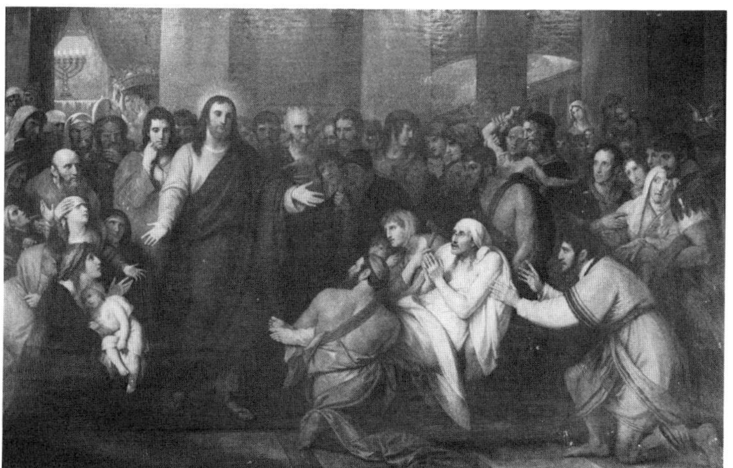

Fig. 4. ***Christ Healing the Sick,*** 1815. Pennsylvania Hospital, Philadelphia, Pennsylvania. Photo: Courtesy of the Pennsylvania Hospital, Philadelphia.

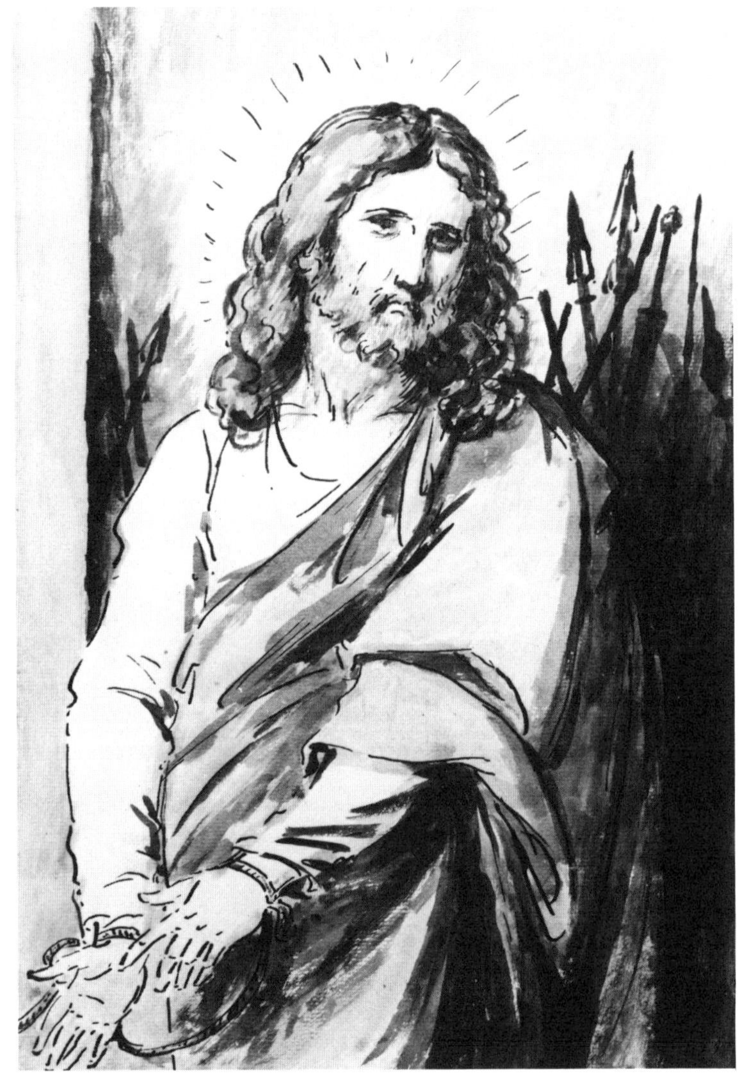

10

10 *Christ Bound*

c. 1819

black and brown ink and wash

11¾ x 7¾

Signed: B. W.

This drawing and three others of the same subject in the Pierpont Morgan Library relate to an oil-and-gouache composition study of *Christ in the Hall of Caiaphas* in the Museum of Fine Arts, Boston. The figure of Christ is quite similar in all six works, the only significant variance being in the position of His hands. Two of the Morgan Library drawings are like the Boston painting in that Christ's hands are crossed. In the Historical Society drawing and the third Morgan Library drawing, Christ's hands are bound but not crossed.

The Boston painting, which is probably a study for a much larger work never executed, has been dated by Allen Staley at around 1814. The Morgan Library drawing most like the Historical Society drawing is inscribed, "The Last design by Benj West-/1819." This inscription was probably added at a later date by Benjamin West, Jr., perhaps after his father's death in March 1820. If this date can be accepted, West apparently continued to make sketches for his *Christ in the Hall of Caiaphas* after completing the Boston study. Based on the position of the hands, the Historical Society drawing probably dates from nearer 1819 than 1814.

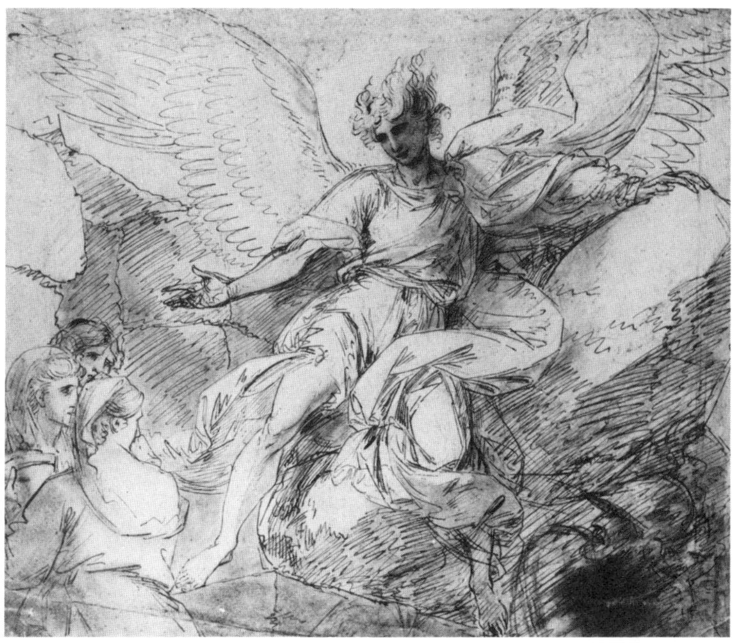

11

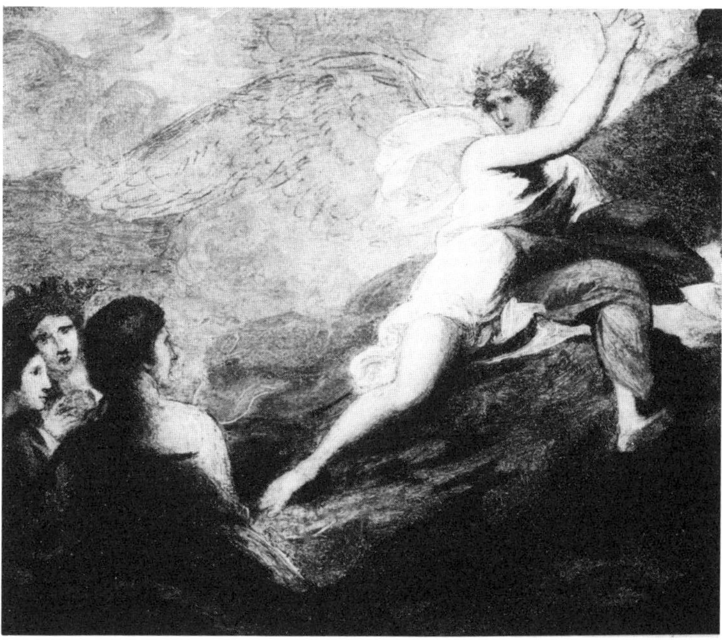

Fig. 5. *The Angel at the Tomb of Christ,* c.1797. Private collection.

11 *The Angel at the Tomb of Christ (The Women at the Sepulchre)*

c. 1797

ink and graphite

16¾ x 19⅝

Allen Staley lists nine paintings of this subject by West. The painting most like the drawing is a privately owned oil sketch on paper (fig. 5). The similarities in the placement and arrangement of the three women is sufficient to suggest that this drawing was a preliminary sketch for the painting. The angel is in roughly the same position, but his gesture and relationship to the tomb is different. In the drawing, he floats, with toes pointed, while he gestures to the empty tomb with his right hand, and rolls away the boulder with his left. In the painting, he sits on the boulder, points down to the open tomb with his left hand and indicates with his right that Christ has arisen. These changes in the angel's gestures profoundly alter the composition, in that the angel is less dominant in the painting and a strong diagonal is created by the angel's outstretched body.

Neither the drawing nor the oil sketch is dated, but an engraving, which copies the painting in every detail, including size, was published in 1797. The oil sketch was probably executed upon request of the printmaker.[10]

12 *Head of Resurrected Christ*

1783

ink

7 x 4¾

Signed: B. West 1783

Inscribed on reverse: Study for the Head of Christ in the cartoon of the Resurrection, painted on glass by Jarvis for St. George's Chapel, Windsor-Benj West

The inscription on the reverse of this drawing describes it as a "Study for the Head of Christ in the cartoon of the Resurrection, painted on glass by Jarvis for St. George's Chapel, Windsor." The chapel window no longer survives; it was dismantled and apparently destroyed in 1863. The cartoon referred to in the inscription was probably West's full-size, 36-by-28-foot cartoon, from which the actual window was painted. This too is lost. West's design for the window is known today primarily through a large full-color oil on canvas study, which is now in the Museo de Arte de Ponce, Puerto Rico.[11] A drawing that closely recreates the entire composition of the painting is in the Delaware Art Museum. In both, Christ, accompanied by an angel, emerges from the open tomb with his eyes heavenward and his arms extended to be met by followers and Roman soldiers, many of whom fall to the ground in amazement. The Historical Society's drawing duplicates the position of Christ's head and shoulders in the other two works.

Neither the painting in Ponce nor the drawing in Delaware is dated. The commission for the window seems to have originated upon George III's suggestion in 1782. Allen Staley dates the painting to around that year but believes that the drawing was done later. West exhibited designs for the window at the Royal Academy exhibition in 1783, the same year the Historical Society drawing is dated. It is not clear when the window was finally installed, but the painting on glass by Thomas Jervais was probably completed in 1786. The full-size cartoon of the design was exhibited in the chapel in October of that year, probably after the window was finished and while the opening in the chapel wall was being made ready to receive it.[12]

Another detail drawing of West's design is owned by Swarthmore College, and five other drawings are in a sketchbook at the Yale Center for British Art.

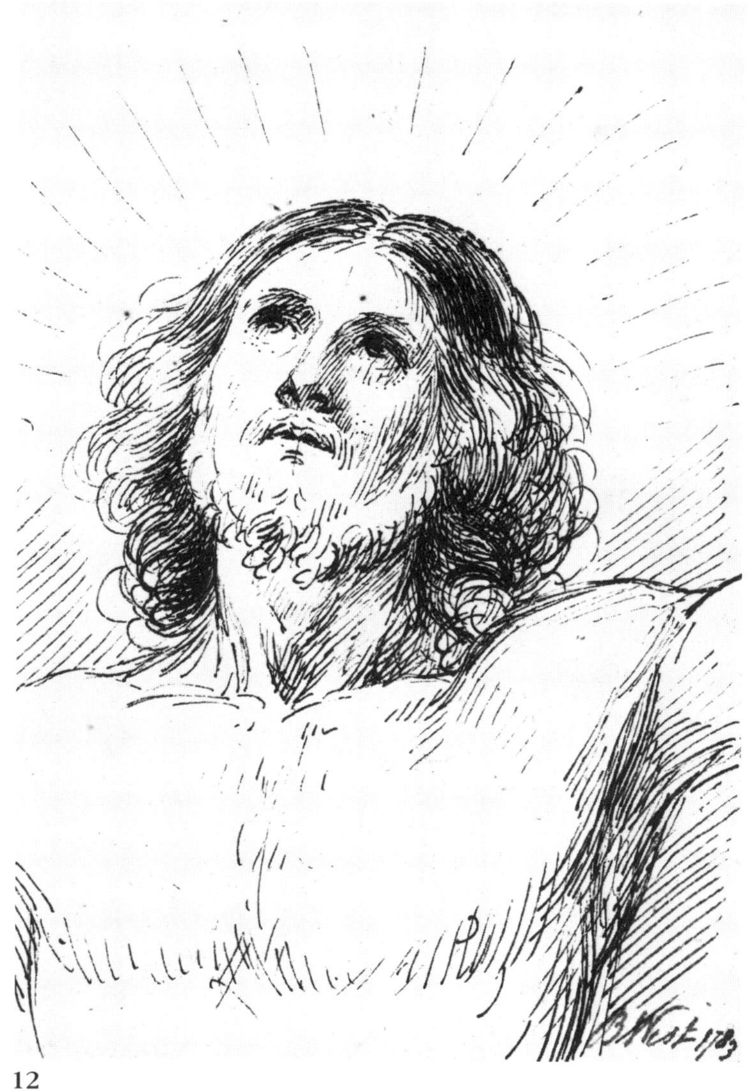

12

13 *The Resurrection*

c. 1786

graphite and white chalk

6¾ x 5⅜

Inscribed on reverse: The Resurrection. A study of the picture which was painted for the Church at Barbadoes Benj West

As the inscription on the reverse of this drawing suggests, it is a study for a painting of the resurrection of Christ for the altar of St. George's Parish Church in Barbados. Henry Frere, president of the Barbados Legislative Council, commissioned the work while on a trip to London. The exact date of the commission is not known but the painting was first exhibited at the Royal Academy exhibition in 1786[13] The drawing is not dated but a date of around 1786 can be assigned in light of these facts.

The arrangement of Christ and the angel in this resurrection resembles the arrangement of the same two figures in West's design for the window of St. George's Chapel at Windsor, done three to four years earlier (see cat. 12). Because the two works depict the same subject with compositional similarities, and were commissioned for churches of the same name, Allen Staley suggests that Frere might have commissioned the Barbados *Resurrection* after seeing West's Windsor Chapel *Resurrection.*[14]

Two other paintings of nearly identical composition to the Barbados *Resurrection* were done by West in later years. One, at Swarthmore College, is signed and dated "B. West 1794" (fig. 6). The second, at Stanford University, is neither signed nor dated. It is probably from a much later period, perhaps near the end of West's life, and might have been finished by another hand.

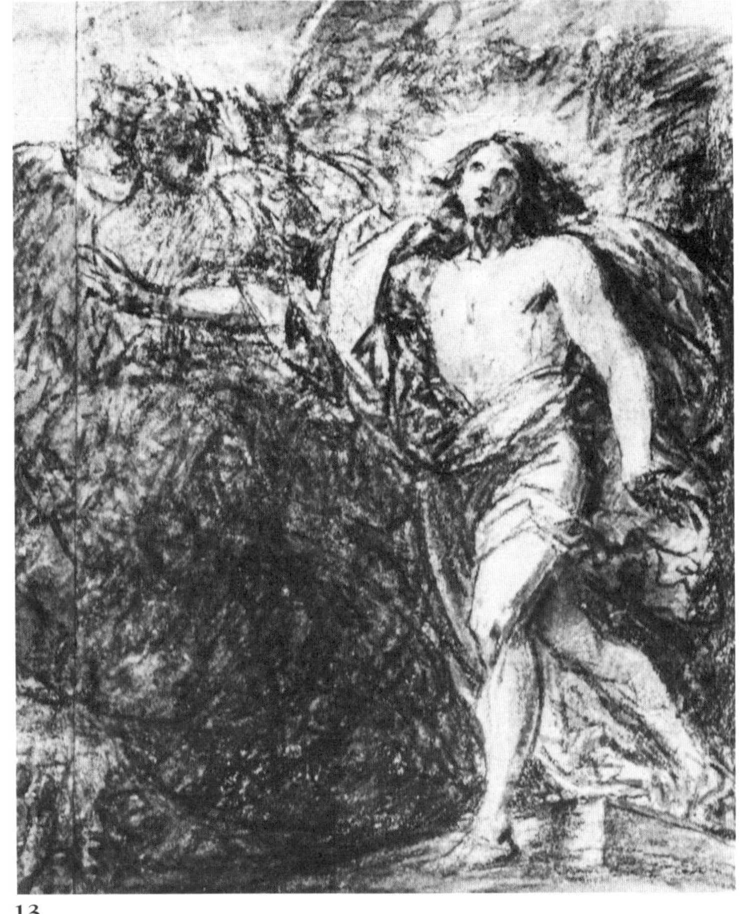

13

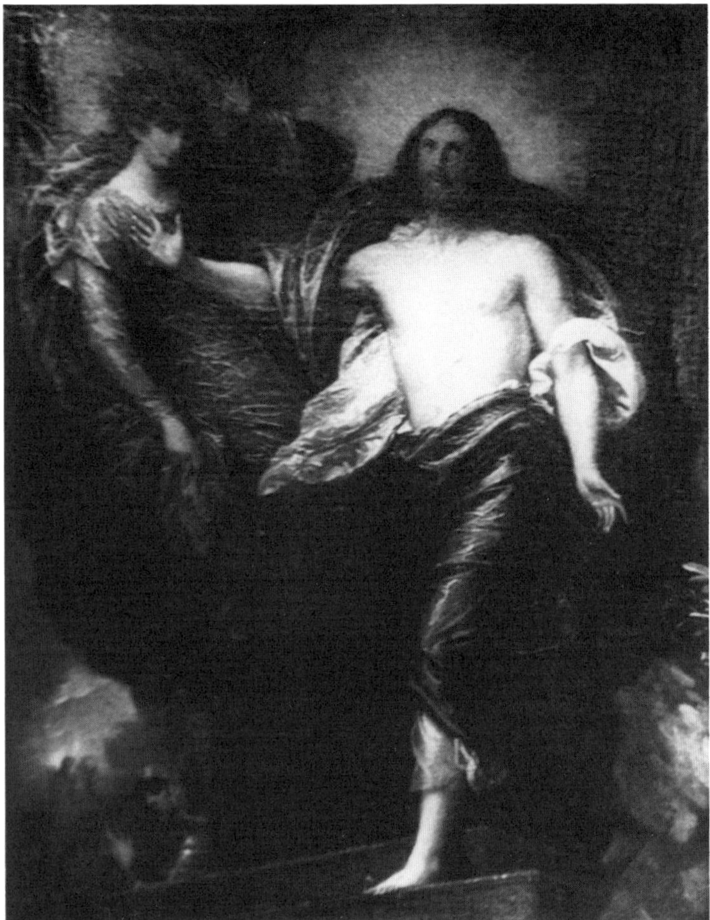

Fig. 6. ***The Resurrection,*** 1794. Swarthmore College, Swarthmore, Pennsylvania.

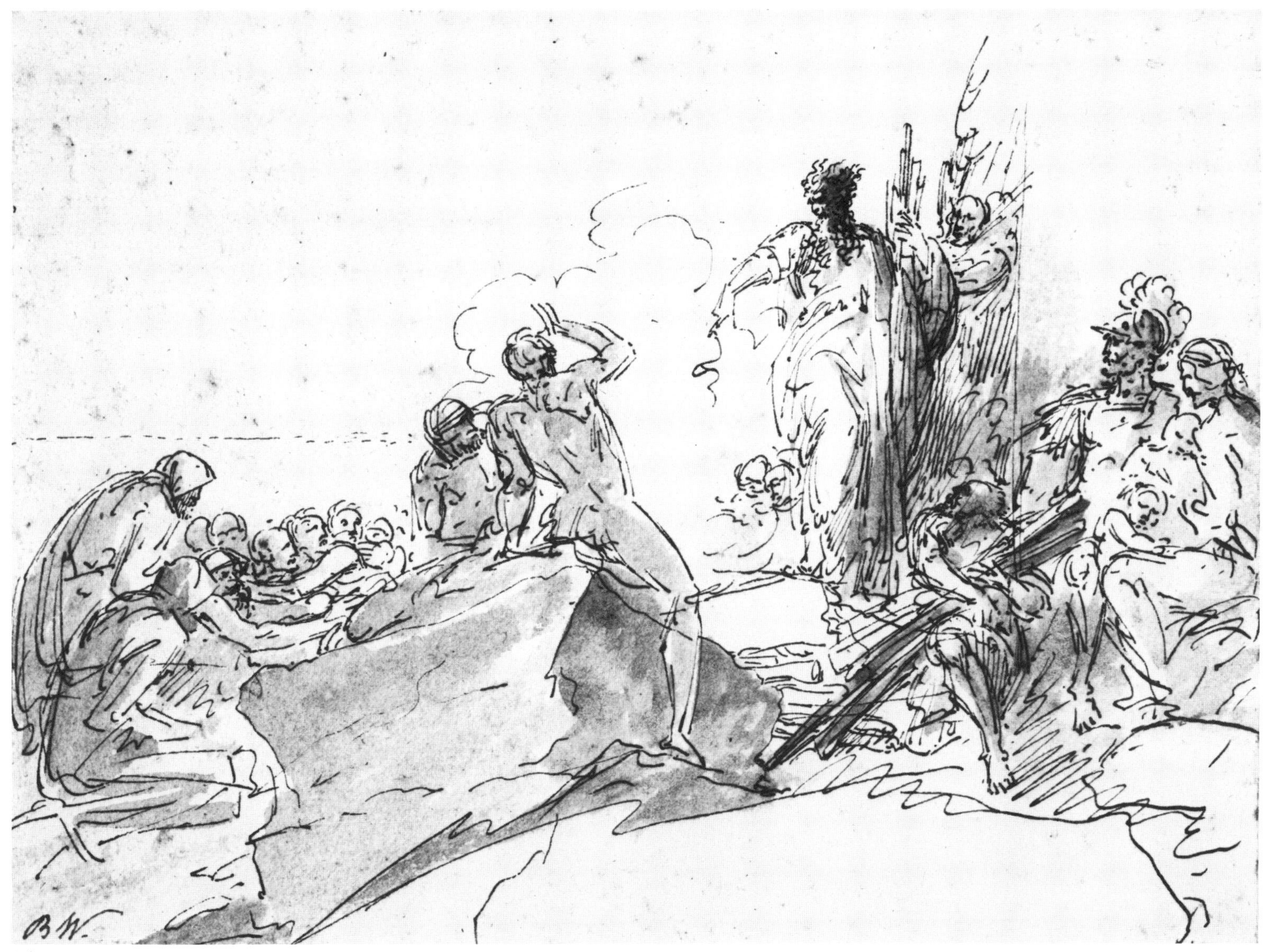

14

14 *St. Paul Shaking the Viper from His Hand after the Shipwreck*

c. 1782

sepia and wash

7½ x 9⅝

Inscribed on reverse: Study for a part of the large Picture of the Shipwreck of St. Paul painted for the chapel in the Hospital at Greenwich. Benj West

As the inscription on the reverse of this drawing indicates, it is a study for West's large altar painting in the Chapel at the Royal Naval Hospital (now College) at Greenwich (fig. 7). The original chapel, built by Christopher Wren and Thomas Ripley, was gutted by fire in 1779 and was in the process of being rebuilt when West received the commission in 1782. The commission included the one large altar painting, designs for numerous other paintings that were executed by Biagio Rebecca, as well as both designs for relief sculpture on the reader's desk and pulpit, and four freestanding pieces for the vestibule. The painting was finished and installed in 1789 as the chapel remodeling neared completion.[15]

The story of the shipwreck of St. Paul is recorded in Acts 28:1–6. Prior to the shipwreck, Paul was arrested in Jerusalem for bringing Greeks into the Temple, a capital offense under Jewish law. Fearing a trial in Jewish court, Paul insisted on a Roman trial. Porcius Festus, governor of Jerusalem, granted his request and sent him to Rome. En route to Rome, the prisoner ship ran aground on the island of Malta. The survivors, assisted by the local inhabitants, built a fire to warm themselves. While Paul was gathering wood for the fire, a viper attached itself to his hand. Seeing this, the natives assumed Paul guilty of a serious crime. They thought although he survived the shipwreck he would not escape justice. When Paul shook the snake off into the fire and suffered no serious injury or illness, the natives thought he must be a god.

The drawing does not closely resemble the composition of the painting, but the figure of Paul, with firewood in his left hand as he

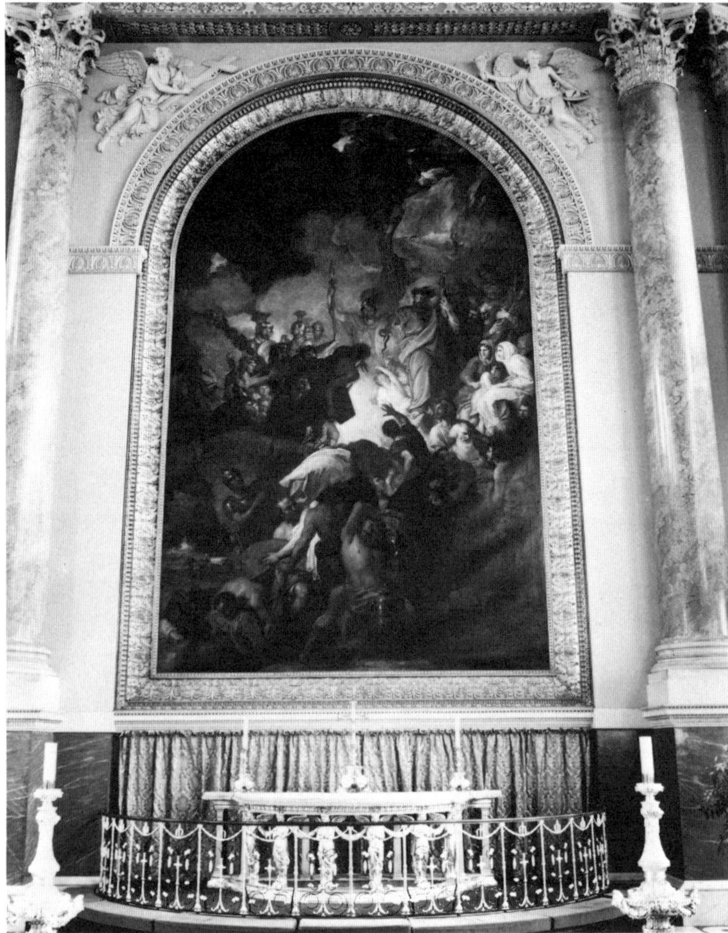

Fig. 7. *St. Paul Shaking the Viper from His Hand after the Shipwreck,* 1789. The Royal Naval College, Greenwich, London, England. Photo: Courtesy of the Director of Greenwich Hospital and The Commander of the College.

shakes the snake clinging to his right hand over the fire, is nearly identical in both works. Other sketches for this painting are in the Art Institute of Chicago and the Museum of Fine Arts, Boston.

15 *St. Matthew*

c. 1785
sepia, sepia wash, and blue wash
8 x 8¼
Inscribed on reverse: St. John Benj West

This figure is St. Matthew
His symbol is the Angel
John Dillenberger, May 5, 1976

16 *St. Mark*

c. 1785
sepia, sepia wash, and blue wash
8 x 8
Inscribed on reverse: St. Mark Benj West

17 *St. Luke*

1785
sepia, sepia wash, and blue wash
8 x 8⅛
Signed: B. West 1785
Inscribed on reverse: St. Luke Benj West

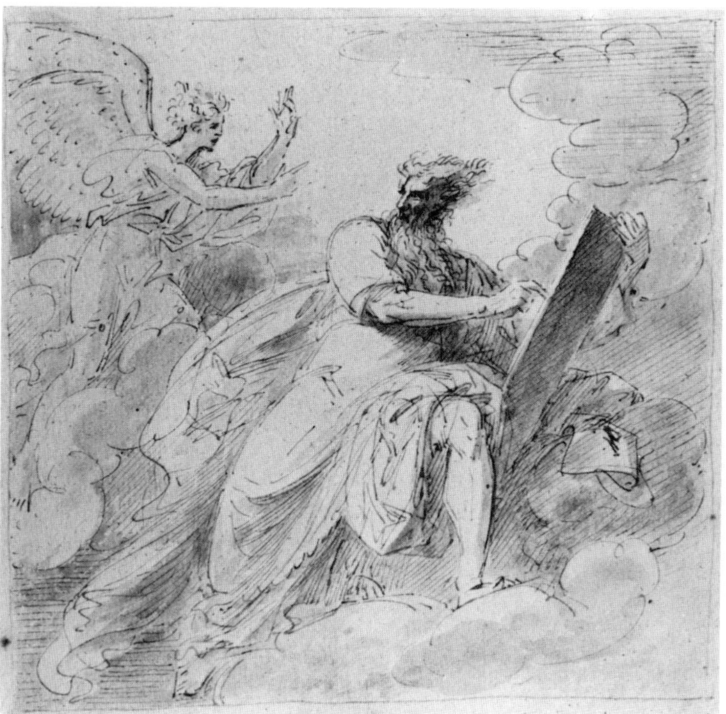

15

18 *St. John*

1785
sepia, sepia wash, and blue wash
8 x 8
Signed: B. West 1785
Inscribed on reverse: St. Matthew Benj West

This figure is St. John
His symbol is an Eagle.
John Dillenberger, May 5, 1976

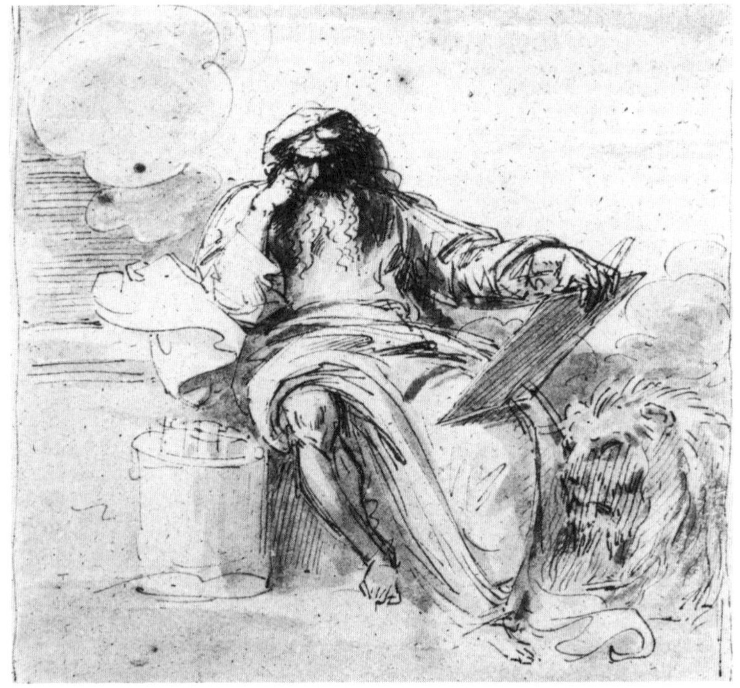

16

These drawings of the Four Evangelists were certainly executed as a set. All four are in sepia with blue wash, and all are within a quarter of an inch of being eight inches square. Each saint is shown with his traditional symbol — Matthew, the winged man; Mark, the lion; Luke, the bull; and John, the eagle. These symbols for the Four Evangelists originated in the early Christian era, with their source in Ezekiel 1:5–14, where the prophet tells of a strange vision of the four beasts. West also continued the tradition of depicting the Evangelists with tablets or scrolls, alluding to their Biblical writings.

There are no known paintings by West of the Four Evangelists, nor is this surprising. The subject is more appropriate for decorative use, and is commonly found in the lunettes or pendentives of domed cathedrals. West's only other known depiction of the Four Evangelists is in a ceiling design apparently meant for the Royal Chapel in

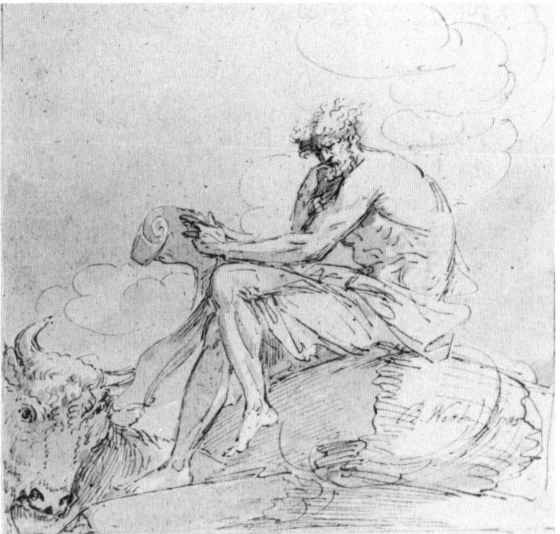

17

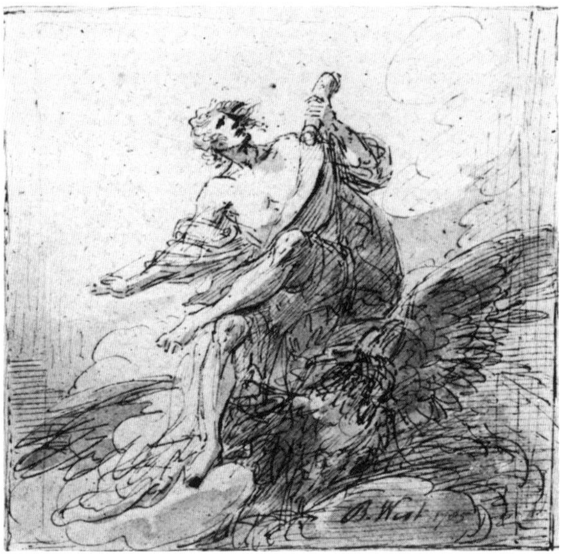

18

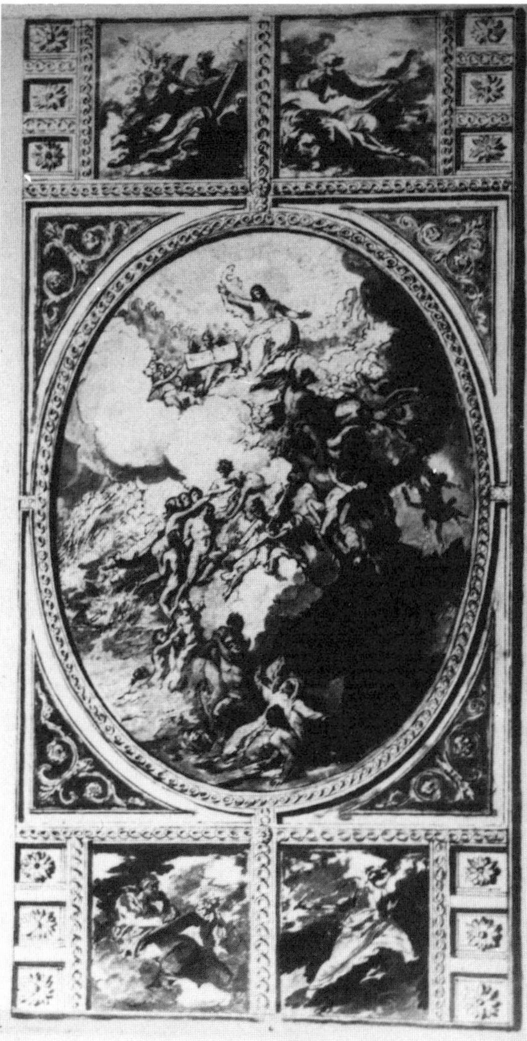

Fig. 8. Benjamin West and Sir William Chambers (?) *Design for the Ceiling of the Royal Chapel, Windsor Castle,* Mr. and Mrs. Erving Wolf.

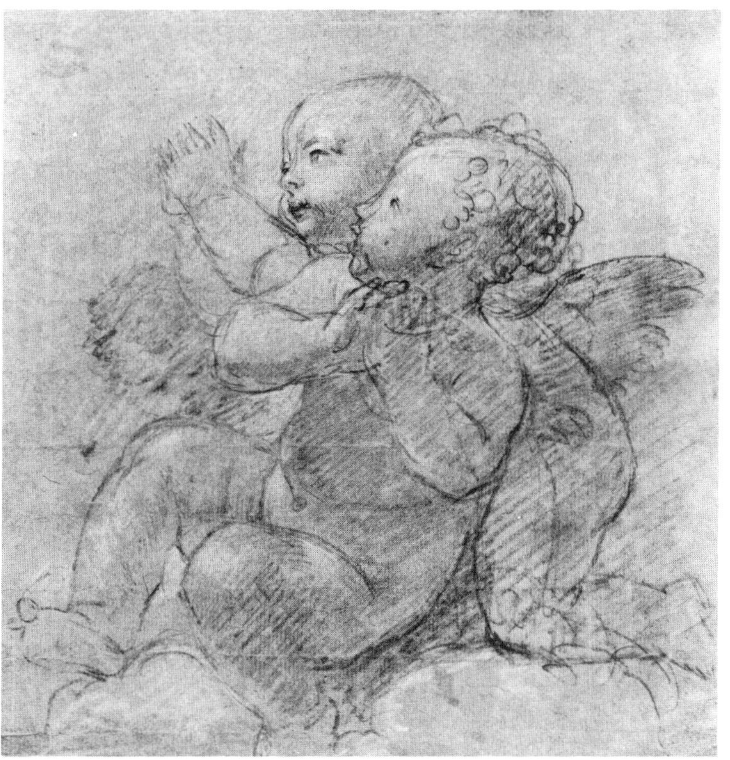

19

Windsor Castle (fig. 8). The Historical Society drawings and the drawings of the Evangelists in the ceiling design are quite similar — the depictions of saints Matthew and John are nearly identical in pose and composition. Furthermore, the square format of the Historical Society drawings is consistent with the design for the proposed ceiling paintings of the saints. West began work on the Royal Chapel project in 1779 and continued to work on it sporadically until 1801. Allen Staley dates the ceiling design to around 1780.[16] Two of the Historical Society drawings, the St. Luke and St. John, are dated "1785," making all four drawings likely studies for the paintings intended for the ceiling of the Royal Chapel but never completed.

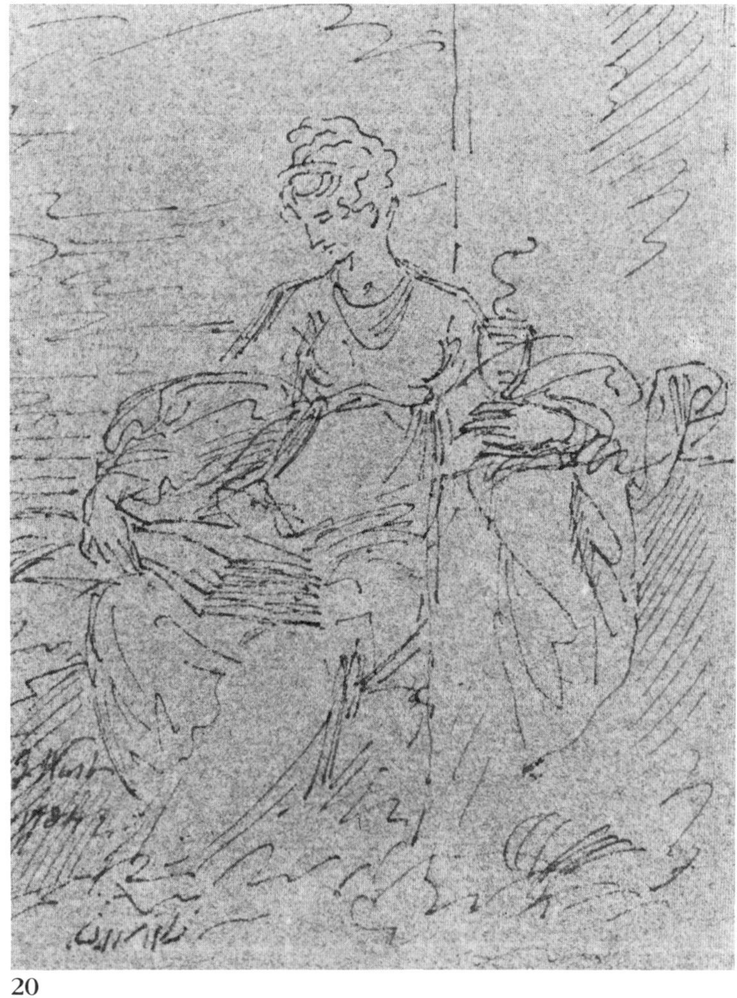
20

19 *Angels*

graphite and white chalk on grey/blue paper

12¼ x 10⅞

The drawing is probably a detail study for a small portion of large religious painting. The figures are identified as angels because they are seated on clouds. Other small winged figures, such as putti or amoretti, are rarely depicted floating on clouds in West's paintings.

This drawing demonstrates West's sensitivity as a draftsman. Though only a preparatory sketch, the drawing shows masterful use of tones for modeling. Graphite is used for the darks, white chalk for highlights, and the colored paper provides the middle tone.

20 *Faith*

1784

sepia on blue paper

5¾ x 4¼

Signed: B. West 1784

Inscribed on reverse: Benj West

The chalice, symbolizing the Eucharist, and the open book, representing the scriptures, are both common attributes of the personification of Faith, one of the three theological virtues along with Hope and Charity. Traditionally, Faith is depicted resting one foot on a block of stone, her unshakable foundation. West alters this convention by placing the block under the arm supporting the chalice instead of under her foot. West's Faith serenely sits reading from the scripture, conveying an air of contentment appropriate for a personification of religious faith.

There are no extant paintings by West of the theological virtues but he is credited with designing the four statues of Faith, Hope, Charity, and Innocence or Meekness, in the vestibule of the Chapel of the Royal Naval College in Greenwich. He received the commission for the design of the sculpture along with numerous other works for the Chapel in 1782.[17] The Historical Society's drawing of Faith is dated 1784. The proximity of these dates supports the possibility that this is an early sketch for the sculpture of Faith.

21 *Hope*

sepia and wash

12¼ x 10

Hope is one of the three theological virtues along with Faith and Charity. Her most common attribute, the anchor, originated from St. Paul's statement in Hebrews 6:19, "We have this (hope) as a sure and steadfast anchor of the soul, a hope that enters into the inner shrine behind the curtain." The anchor in West's drawing appears to rest upon a block of stone which, when seen with personifications of Faith, another of the three virtues, represents her unshakable foundation. West effectively enhances the theme of Hope by depicting his personification optimistically gazing up at a shaft of sunlight breaking through the clouds.

West apparently did not paint the three virtues, but he is believed to have designed the four statues of Faith, Hope, Charity, and Innocence or Meekness, in the vestibule of the Chapel of the Royal Naval College at Greenwich.[18] This drawing was possibly done in preparation for the design of the sculpture of Hope, but its attention to detail and concentration on light make it an unlikely design for a sculpture.

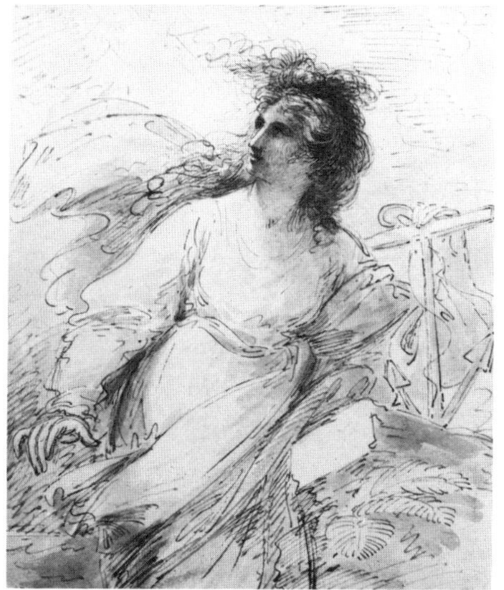

21

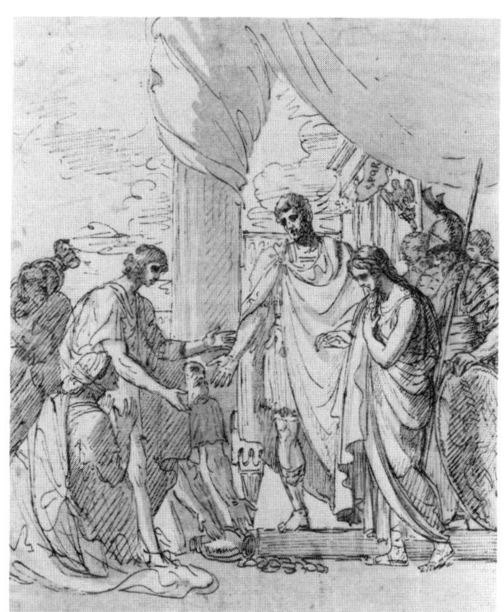

22

22 *The Continence of Scipio*

ink and wash

9 x 7¼

Inscribed on reverse: The Continence of Scipio Benj. West

The story of Scipio Africanus returning a captured Carthaginian maiden to her family and fiancé, along with a dowry of the gold brought for her ransom, was recorded by Livy and Valerius Maximus. However, according to Allen Staley, the subject was so popular among eighteenth-century painters that West probably did not need to refer to a literary source.

The one painting by West of this subject that is known, now in the Fitzwilliams Museum, bears little resemblance to the Historical Society's drawing. A second painting of the subject might have been painted — the title *Continence of Scipio* appears in the Royal Academy exhibition records for both 1766 and 1771. The 1766 listing is believed to represent the Fitzwilliams painting, but no other record of the 1771 painting has been found. It is possible that the Fitzwilliams painting was exhibited twice; however, such practice was expressly prohibited by Academy rules.[19] The Historical Society drawing supports the possibility of there having been a second painting.

Because of its size, format, and subject this drawing could be a companion to the Historical Society's drawing of *Chryseis Returned to Her Father* (cat. 34). Both drawings depict the reuniting of a young woman with her family. The painting done after the *Chryseis* drawing does have a companion (both paintings are in the New York Historical Society collection), but the companion depicts *Aeneas and Creusa,* not *The Continence of Scipio.*[20]

23 *Agrippina with Her Children Going through the Roman Camp*

1780s

sepia on blue paper

12¾ x 9

Inscribed on reverse: Agrippina with Her Children going through the Roman Camp when in a state of mutiny.

Agrippina was the daughter of Agrippa, granddaughter of Augustus, and wife of Germanicus, the nephew and adopted son of the Emperor Tiberius. According to the *Annals* of Tacitus (Book I), Agrippina accompanied Germanicus on his campaigns against the Germanic tribes. When a mutiny broke out among the Roman troops, Germanicus ordered Agrippina to take refuge with the local Treveri (residents of Trier). Her departure sufficiently shamed the mutinous troops so that they begged her to stay and eventually abandoned the revolt.[21]

West depicts Agrippina carrying her infant son, Caligula, and accompanied by two attendants as she makes her way through the Roman camp. Soldiers, some kneeling, plead with her not to leave. Although the drawing is not elaborate, it is refined and sensitively drawn. With an economy of line West conveys the emotions of each participant in the scene. The child clings to his mother's breast in fear. The attendants, with hands folded in prayer, cringe behind their mistress. The soldiers express remorse and concern in their faces and through their gestures. The elegantly elongated Agrippina towers over the scene in controlled sorrow, while in the background the mutiny continues in another area of the camp.

West apparently did not paint this subject, but two other drawings of the subject survive, one in a private collection and one at the Pierpont Morgan Library. Both drawings differ from the Historical Society's version in composition, but the privately owned drawing repeats many of its details.[22] The Morgan Library drawing is a small rough black chalk sketch with none of the detail of the others. Of the three, only the privately owned drawing is dated, at 1785. Ruth Kraemer has dated the Historical Society drawing to the 1780s on the basis of its style.[23]

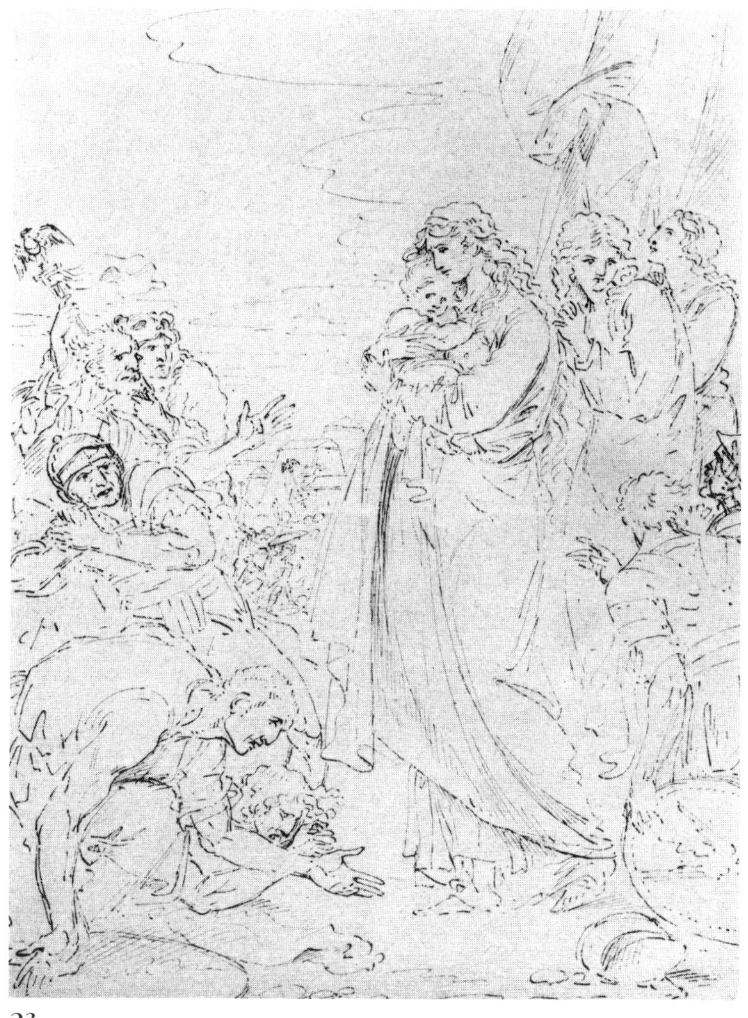

23

24 *Segestes and His Daughter before Germanicus*

c. 1773

ink and sepia wash

7⅝ x 6¾

Signed B. W.

Inscribed on reverse: Segestes and His Daughter before Germanicus Benj. West

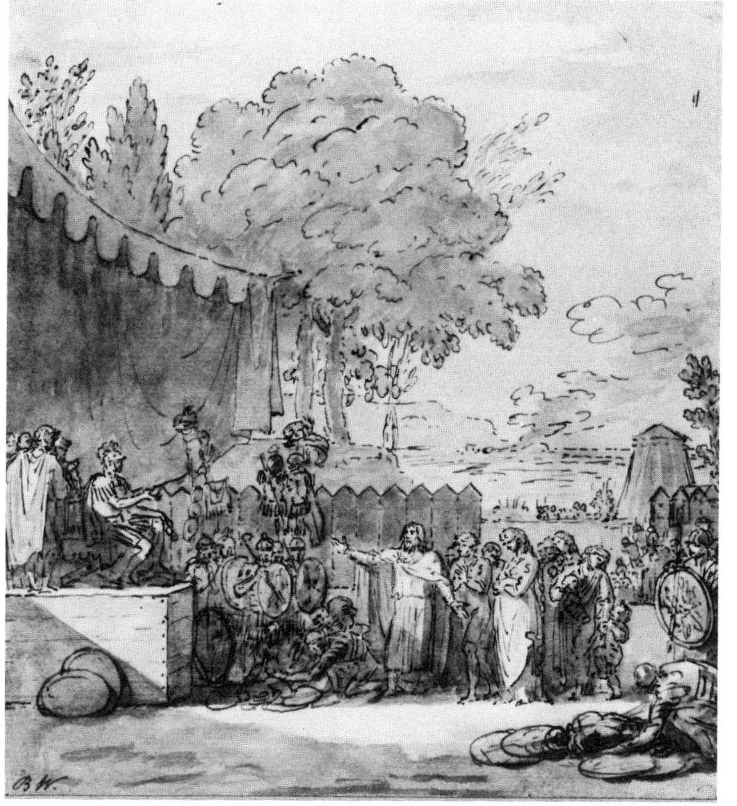

24

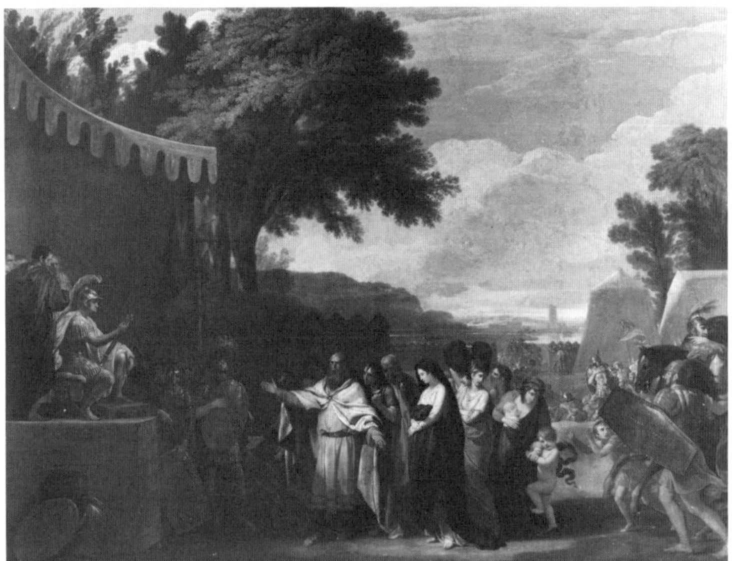

Fig. 9. *Segestes and His Daughter before Germanicus,* 1773. Her Majesty the Queen

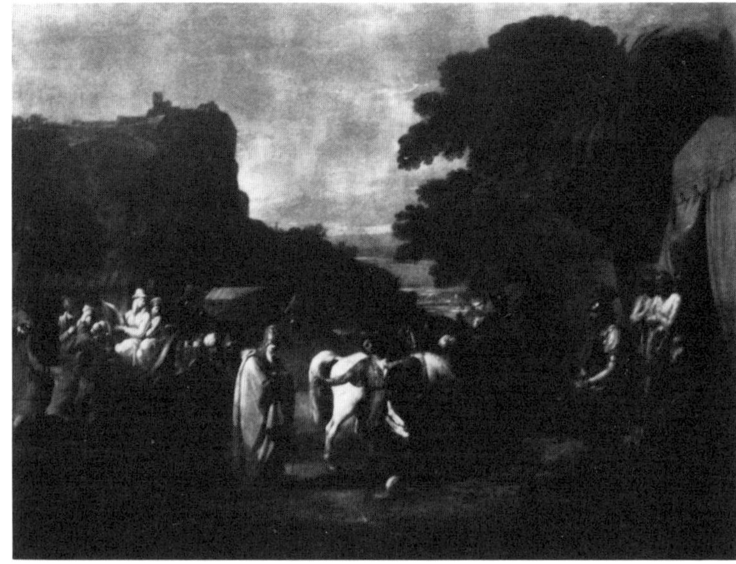

Fig. 10. *The Family of the King of Armenia Before Cyrus 1773.* Her Majesty the Queen

After his troops abandoned their mutiny, Germanicus intervened in a dispute between two rival Germanic leaders, Segestes, who was a friend of the Romans, and Arminius, who was an enemy. Germanicus rescued Segestes, and in the process took a number of Arminius' followers prisoner, including Segestes' son and his daughter, who was the pregnant wife of Arminius. West depicts Segestes appealing to Germanicus to spare his children. According to the *Annals* of Tacitus (Book I), Segestes recounted his loyality to Rome, asked for his son's pardon, and submitted to Germanicus:

> As for my daughter, I admit that it is by compulsion she has been brought here. It will be for you to consider which fact weighs most with you, that she is with child by Arminius or that she owes her being to me.[24]

Germanicus responded by promising safety to Segestes' family.

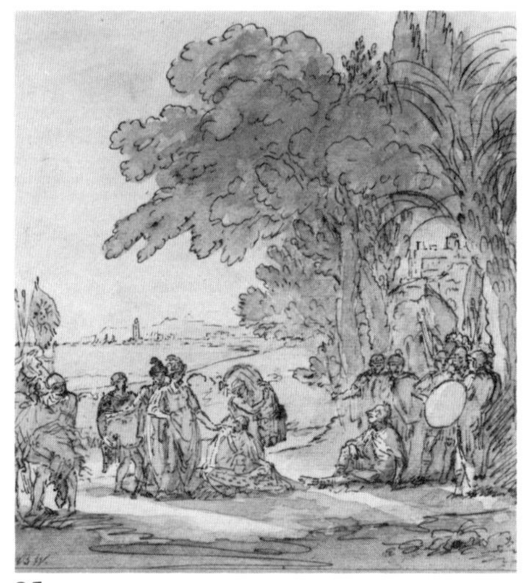

25

The drawing is not dated, but a painting of the same subject with a nearly identical composition, except in a horizontal format, is dated "1773," (fig. 9). West did the painting, now in the collection of Her Majesty the Queen, for George III as a companion piece to a second painting of a similar subject, *The Family of the King of Armenia before Cyrus.*[25] The Historical Society's drawing of *Segestes and His Daughter before Germanicus* also has a companion drawing, and its composition bears some resemblance to *The Family of the King of Armenia before Cyrus,* but the subject is *Agesilaus Rejecting the Magnificence Offered Him by the Egyptian Envoys* (cat. 25).

25 *Agesilaus Rejecting the Magnificence Offered Him by the Egyptian Envoys*

c. 1773

ink and sepia wash

7½ x 6¾

Signed: BW

Inscribed on reverse: Agesilaus rejecting the Magnificence offered him by the Egyptian Envoys Benj West

Inscribed on front: Sysilaus Bearing Gifts

This drawing was intended as a companion to the Historical Society's drawing of *Segestes and His Daughter before Germanicus* (cat. 24). The drawings are of the same size, the same media and depict similar subjects. In both scenes one party stands before a more authoritative power appealing for favors. West's painting of *Segestes and His Daughter before Germanicus,* done after the Historical Society's drawing, does have a companion painting. It is not *Agesilaus and the Egyptian Envoys,* but a third very similar subject, *The Family of the King of Armenia Before Cyrus* (fig. 10). Both paintings were done for George III in 1773, and remain in the collection of Her Majesty the Queen.[26] The drawing of *Agesilaus and the Egyptian Envoys* and the painting of *The King of Armenia Before Cyrus* share similarities in the grouping of figures, the position of the palm tree, the servant restraining the horse, and the exotically dressed figure standing before the helmeted warrior. But they illustrate two different historic events. These similarities in composition and differences in subject suggest that West executed the two Historical Society drawings in preparation for the two paintings for George III, later replaced his proposed subject of Agesilaus, but retained much of his original composition

Agesilaus was the younger son of Archidamus II. He overcame his slight build and lame leg to reign as King of Sparta from around 399 to 360 B.C. His aggressive military leadership and simple life-style more than compensated for his frail body. He was known as the best general and citizen Sparta ever had. Agesilaus was King during the period of Sparta's greatest power but his constant crusades drained the country's treasury. The scene depicted in West's drawing took place late in his life, when he led a band of mercenaries to Egypt. Agesilaus intended to support Tachos in exchange for money needed to finance Sparta's wars. However, when the Egyptians, who knew of Agesilaus by reputation, saw the lame, frail eighty-year-old man, they mocked him and he was not given supreme command as he expected. As a result Agesilaus joined a revolt against Tachos and helped the conspirators gain control of Egypt. West's drawing apparently depicts Egyptians offering Agesilaus riches to return to the side of Tachos.

26 *Agrippina with Her Children Weeping over the Ashes of Germanicus*

1771

graphite

12⅝ x 9¾

Signed: B. West 1771

Germanicus, Agrippina's husband, died during a visit to the eastern provinces after his successful campaigns against the Germanic tribes. According to the *Annals* of Tacitus (Book III), it was widely believed

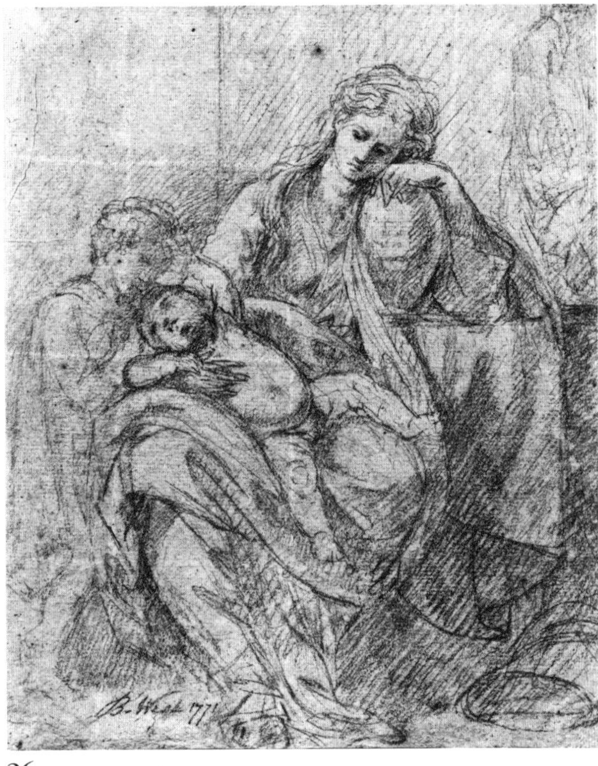

26

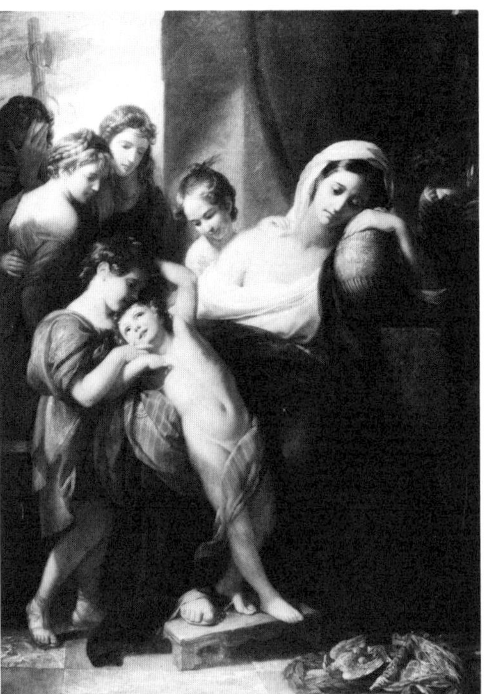

Fig. 11. *Agrippina, Surrounded by Her Children, Weeping over the Ashes of Germanicus,* c.1773. John and Mable Ringling Museum of Art, Sarasota, Florida.

that he was poisoned by Calpurnius Piso, Governor of Syria, with the consent of the Emperor Tiberius, who feared his nephew as a rival to his crown. Agrippina weeping over her husband's ashes is not a scene specifically described by Tacitus; however, he does say that before returning to Rome with Germanicus' ashes Agrippina spent a few days on the island of Corcyra (Corfu) to compose herself, since she was "wild with grief."[27] Allen Staley suggests that West's inspiration for the subject came from a painting titled *Agrippina Weeping over the Ashes of Germanicus* by Gavin Hamilton, which was exhibited at the Royal Academy in 1770 (the location of this work is now unknown).[28] The Historical Society's drawing is signed and dated "B. West 1771." An undated painting with a very similar composition, now in the John and Mable Ringling Museum of Art at Sarasota, Florida, was first exhibited in 1773 (fig. 11).

Both the drawing and the painting depict Agrippina resting her head and hand on an urn containing the ashes of Germanicus (in the painting the urn is inscribed OSSA/GERMANICI/C. AUG.). In the drawing a nude child, presumably her son, Caligula, sprawls across her lap and reaches his hand toward the head of another child standing alongside. The child is larger in the painting and stands in front of Agrippina. Additional background figures and other details were added to the painting.

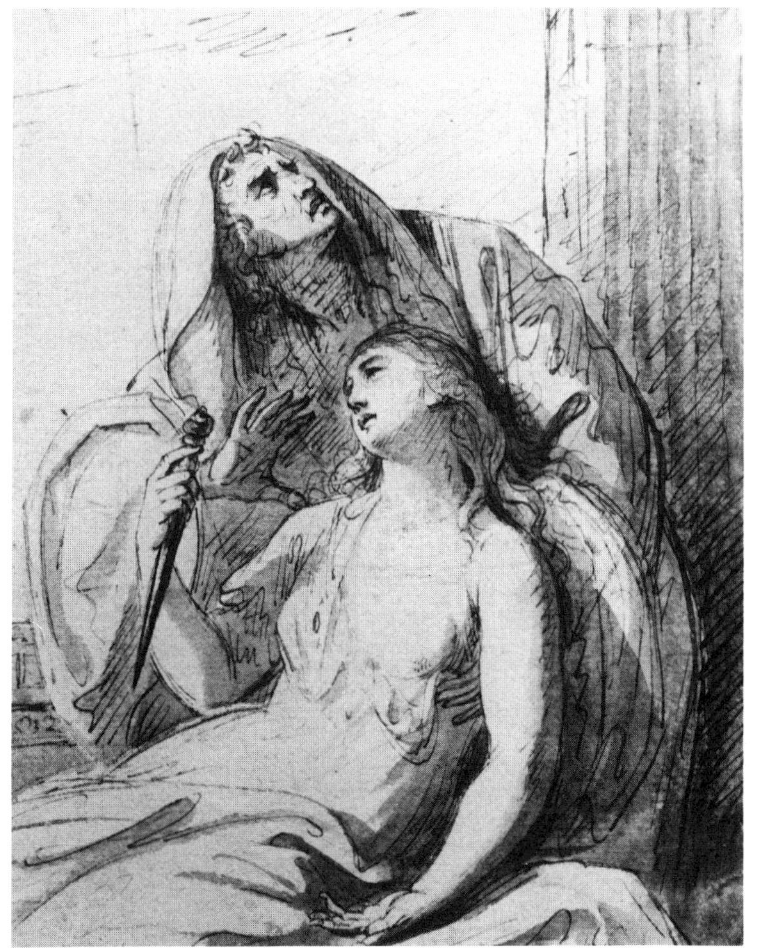

27

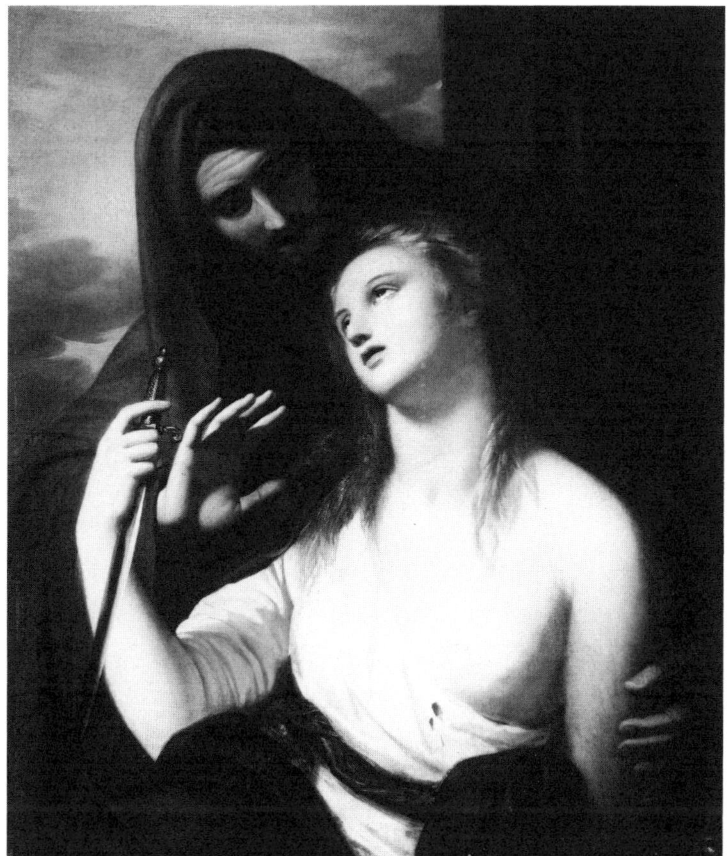

Fig. 12. *Paetus and Arria,* 1770. Private Collection.

27 *Paetus and Arria*

c. 1770

ink and wash

7⅝ x 5⅞

Inscribed on reverse: Patus and Arria Benj West

The story of Paetus and Arria is recorded in the *Letters* of Pliny (Book III, 16). Paetus, having been sentenced to death by Claudius for participating in a revolt against the Emperor, was told to choose his means of execution. While he pondered his decision, his wife, Arria, seized a dagger, plunged it into her breast, and offered it to him saying, "It does not hurt, Paetus."

A privately owned painting of this subject in a very similar composition (fig. 12), is signed "Benj. West 1770." One significant difference between the drawing and the painting is the position of Paetus' head. However, an X-ray of the painting reveals that he was originally painted looking up, as he does in the drawing. Allen Staley points out the similarity between the Arria in the drawing and Lucretia in Gavin Hamilton's *Oath of Brutus* (fig. 2),[29] and suggests West was influenced by the painting. A drawing of the figure of Arria is at Swarthmore College.

28 *Paetus and Arria*

c. 1780

sepia, wash, and blue wash

22 x 15⅝

West produced three distinctly different paintings of *Paetus and Arria.*[30] Two of these compositions are represented in the Historical Society's collection of drawings (see cat. 27). The painting done after this drawing is lost and is known only from a mezzotint done after the painting (fig. 13). The mezzotint by Valentine Green was published May 1, 1781.[31] The drawing and the mezzotint are very similar in nearly every detail.

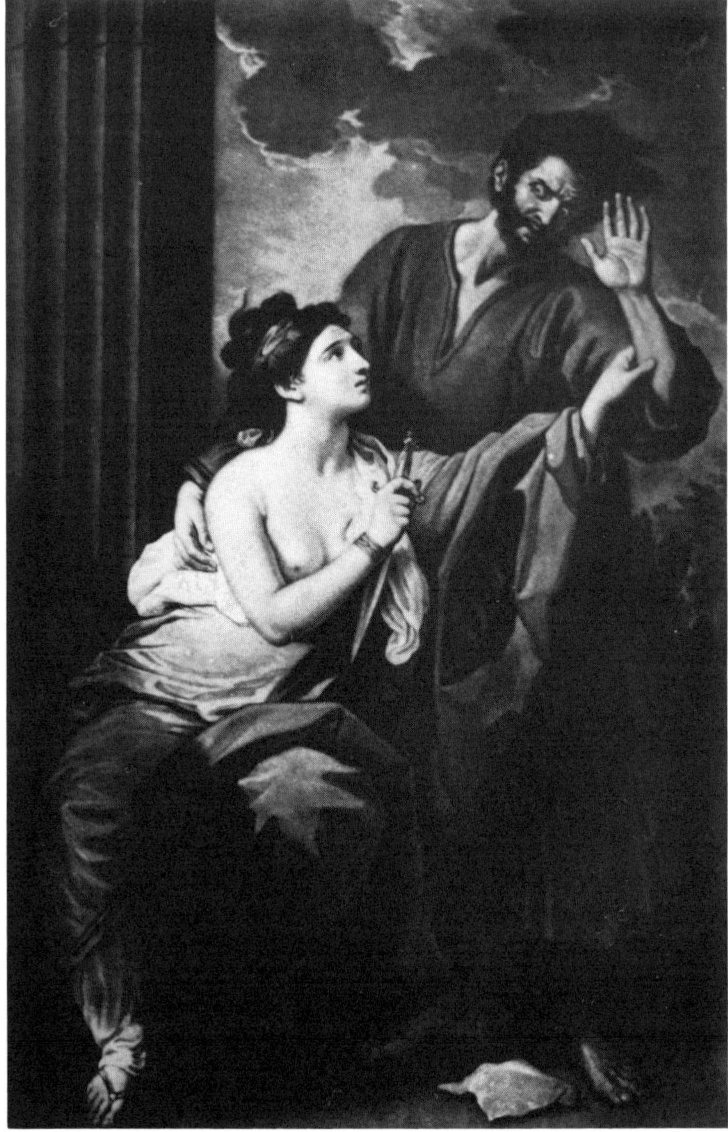

Fig. 13. Valentine Green, *Paetus and Arria,* 1781, mezzotint after West.

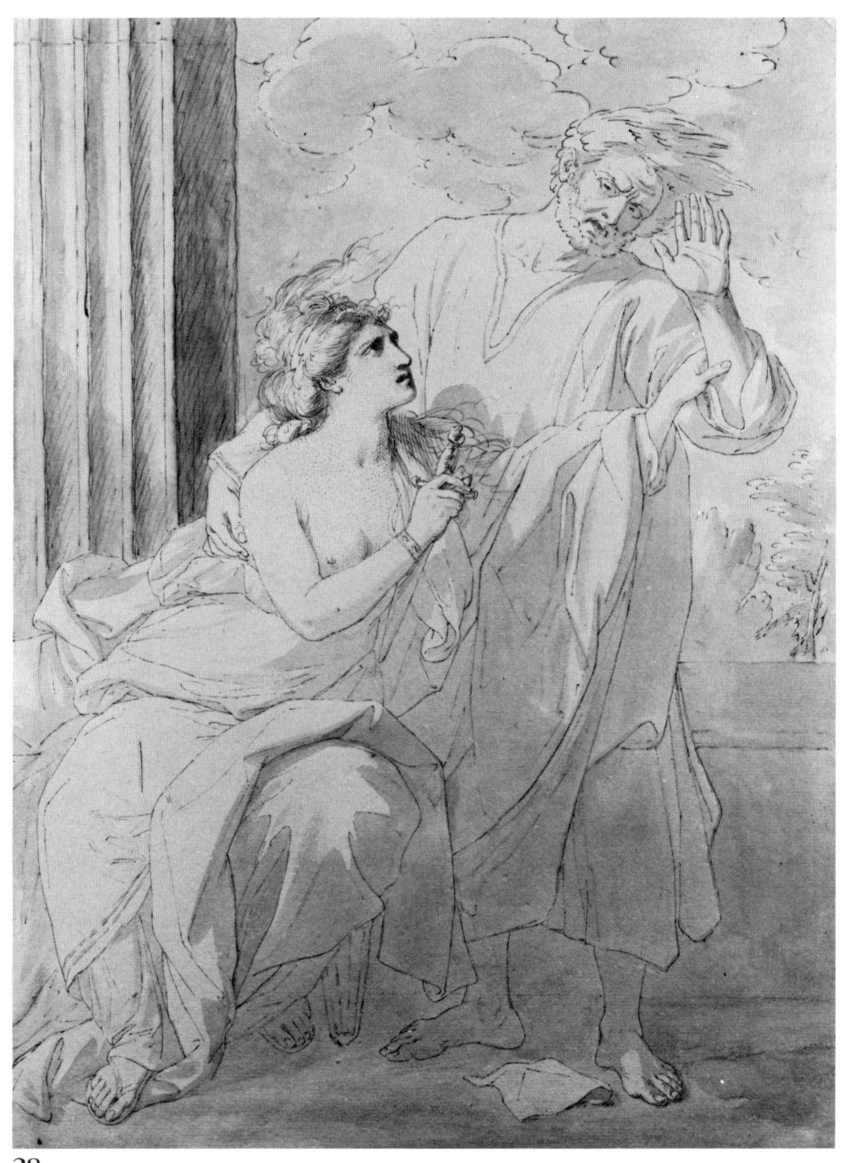

28

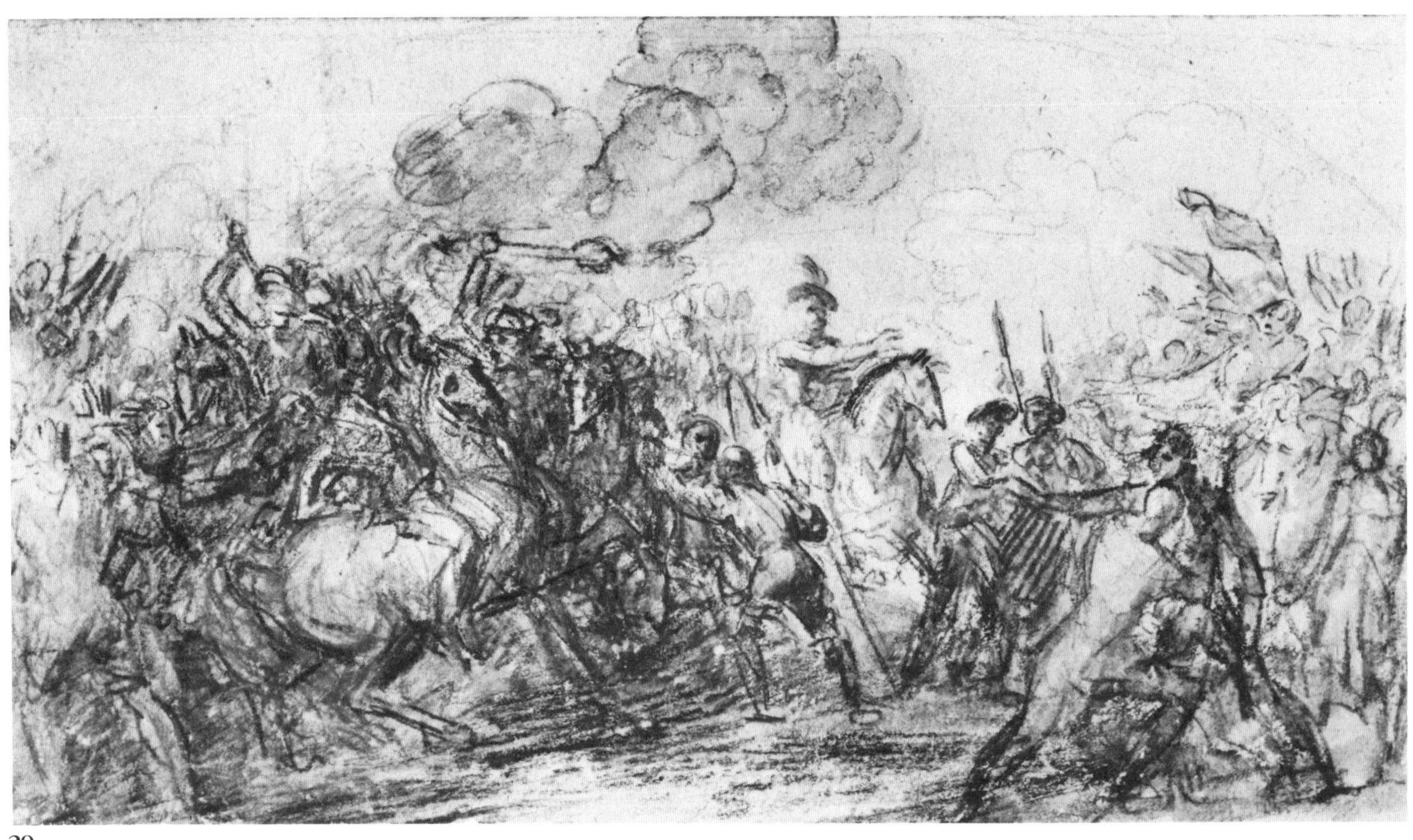

29

29 *The Death of Wat Tyler*

graphite and sepia wash

$6\frac{3}{4}$ x 12

Wat Tyler was the leader of the great English peasant rebellion of 1381. The rebellion began in the spring of that year, when villagers in Fobbing, Corringham, and Stanford in southwest Essex refused to pay a heavy poll tax passed by Parliament in December 1380. Fueled by the royal council's feeble efforts to restore discipline, the rebellion escalated and quickly spread throughout Essex and into neighboring Kent. Wat Tyler joined the uprising when it reached his native village of Maidstone in Kent. Under his leadership, the rebels marched to London to present a list of demands to King Richard II.

The peasants occupied the capital city, and even barricaded the King and members of his council in the Tower of London for three days until Richard met with Tyler at Smithfield on June 15. Tyler's demands on that day were enormous — he not only demanded the abolition of serfdom but also the abolition of all lordship except the King. His demeanor was rude and aggressive. As he defiantly waved his dagger and charged his horse among the King's attendants, he was mortally wounded by William Walworth, Lord Mayor of London.[32] Fourteen-year-old King Richard defused the potentially explosive situation by shouting to the angry peasant mob, "You are in need of a leader! I will be your leader!" Richard led them away from London while Walworth summoned military forces in the city, which forced the peasants to disband.[33]

The legend of Wat Tyler as a leader of rebels against the aristocracy of England survived until West's day. In fact, a three-act dramatic poem glorifying Tyler was written in 1794 by Robert Southey.[34] Tributes to Wat Tyler in any form would not have been popular among loyalists. Southey's poem was surreptitiously published in 1817 by his enemies to disgrace the then–Poet Laureate of England[35]. None of West's three sketches of *The Death of Wat Tyler* in the Historical Society are dated, so no direct connection to Southey's poem can be made. Nor are any of the drawings signed; but, as Court History Painter to King George III, West's choice to sketch this subject at all is quite surprising.

The drawing depicts the scene at Smithfield the moment of the attack on Tyler. The rebel leader is shown slumping backward from his horse under the maces of the royal guards in the left half of the drawing. Near the center, King Richard motions as he speaks to Tyler's followers. From the few details visible in the drawing, costumes seem to be consistent with the period (i.e., the shirt and britches on the man in the center and the plume in Richard's hat). This point is of interest when considering the classical garb in the other two drawings of this subject in the Historical Society collection.

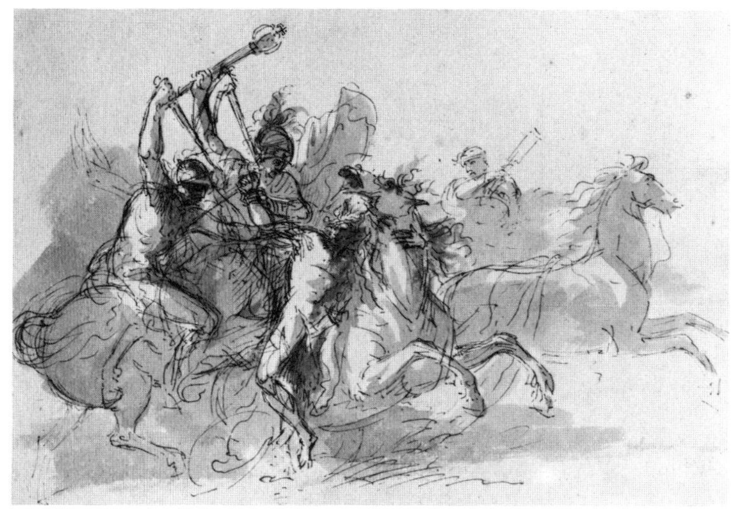

30

30 *The Death of Wat Tyler (?)*

ink and sepia wash

9⅝ x 14¼

A label affixed to this drawing identifies the subject as *The Death of Wat Tyler* (see cat. 29). The arrangement of figures vaguely resembles the left half of cat. 29, which was inscribed, "the Death of Wat Tyler" by Benjamin West, Jr. An important difference, however, is the classical setting implied by the nude figure and by the helmets on the attackers. It is unusual for West to classicize a nonclassical historic event; however, if this drawing does depict the story of Wat Tyler, West might have wished to disguise the subject due to its politically sensitive nature.

The drawing is clearly a working sketch — note the multiple positions of the attackers' arms, and the horse's leg and hoof visible within the hindquarter of the horse on the far left. It is neither signed nor dated.

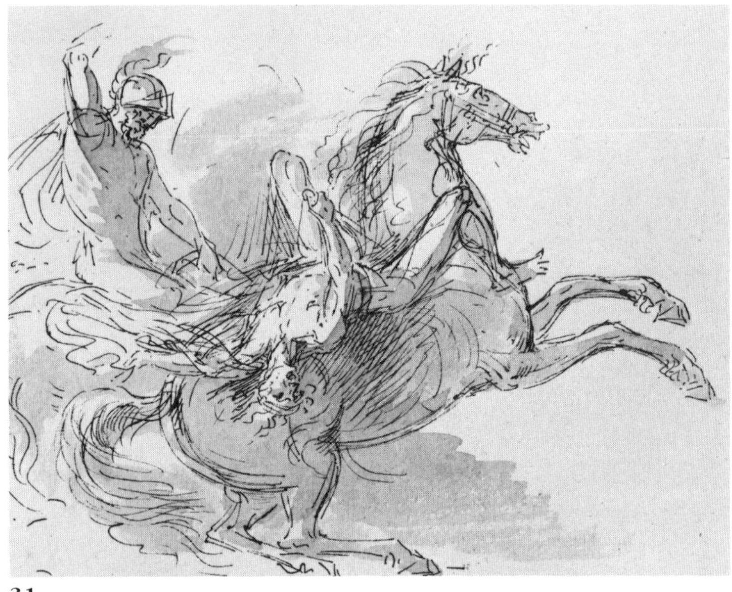

31

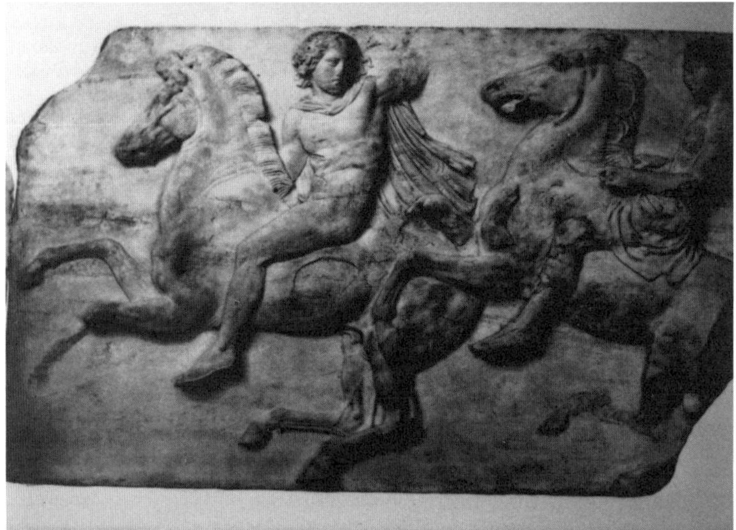

Fig. 14. ***Horseman,*** from the West frieze of the Parthenon. British Museum, London, England.

31 *The Death of Wat Tyler (?)*

ink and wash

7⅞ x 9⅞

Inscribed on reverse: Benj West

This drawing is similar to cat. 30 in media, style, and subject and might also depict the death of Wat Tyler. Perhaps the most interesting aspect of this sketch, though, is its resemblance to the horsemen on the frieze from the north and west sides of the Parthenon (fig. 14). Segments of these ancient reliefs were brought to England by Thomas Bruce, Earl of Elgin, in 1804 and put on display at his estate in 1807. West spent three weeks studying and sketching the marbles in the fall of that year.[36] The drawing is not dated, but its similarities to the reliefs, including the position and proportions of the horse and the nude rider, and the position of the attacker's raised arm, are sufficient to suggest probable influence.

MODERN LITERATURE

32 *Rinaldo and Armida*

1788

sepia

11 x 16

Signed: B. West 1788

The story of Rinaldo and Armida is from Torquato Tasso's epic poem *Gerusalemme Liberata* (Jerusalem Delivered), a romantic account of the first Christian Crusade, which ended with the capture of Jerusalem in 1099 and the establishment of a Christian kingdom. In Tasso's poem, Armida was a virgin witch sent by Satan to seek revenge against the Christian crusaders. Rinaldo was a young Christian prince who converted Armida's hatred to love. The passage depicted in the draw-

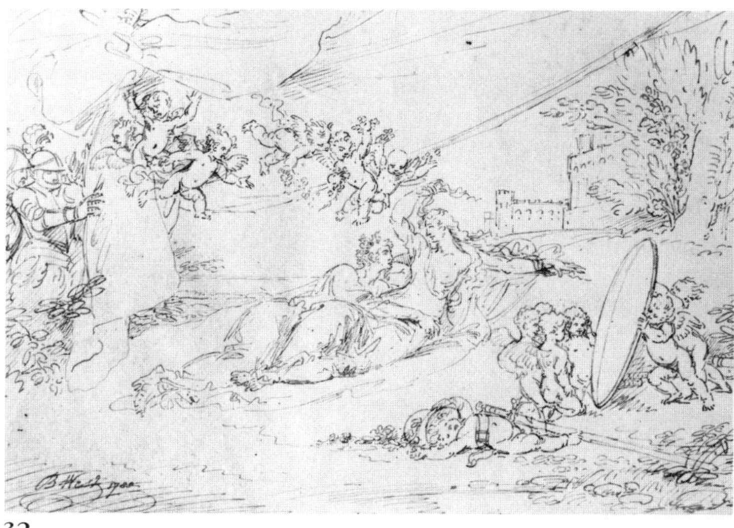

32

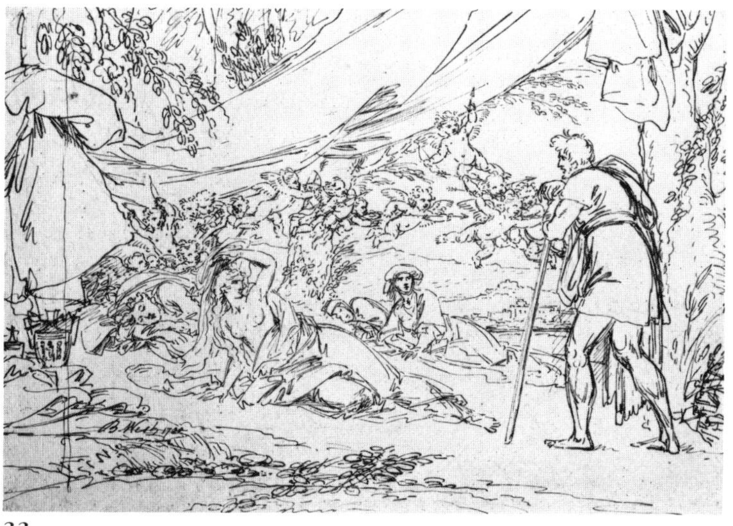

33

ing describes the lovers reclining on Armida's island paradise with her castle in the distance. Rinaldo sees the love on his own face reflected in Armida's eyes. He holds a mirror before her face so she can experience the same pleasure as she plays with her hair. The lovers are discovered in this position by two of Rinaldo's fellow warriors who have come looking for him.

The drawing is consistent with its literary source in every respect except one. Instead of Rinaldo holding a mirror for Armida, the two see their love reflected in each other's eyes. West supplements this theme with a group of amoretti who playfully see their reflection in Rinaldo's shield.

West did at least three paintings of this scene, but neither the composition nor the date of the drawing correspond to any of the paintings. Another Historical Society drawing of a similar subject, *Cymon and Iphigenia* (cat. 33), is also dated "1788." The two compositions were probably planned as companion paintings but were never executed.

33 *Cymon and Iphigenia*

1788

sepia

12½ x 18¼

Signed: B. West 1788

The story of Cymon and Iphigenia originates from the *Decameron,* by Giovanni Boccaccio, but was retold in English in John Dryden's *Fables,* first published in 1700. In both sources, Cymon is a handsome but dull-witted son of a wealthy nobleman. After being sent to live with the peasants in the country, he happened upon Iphigenia and her companions sleeping near a fountain. Struck by her beauty, he fell in love, and after several twists of fate they were married. Iphigenia's love eventually transformed the crude youth into an accomplished and polished gentlemen.

Cymon and Iphigenia was a popular subject among painters of the seventeenth and eighteenth centuries. West painted the theme at least

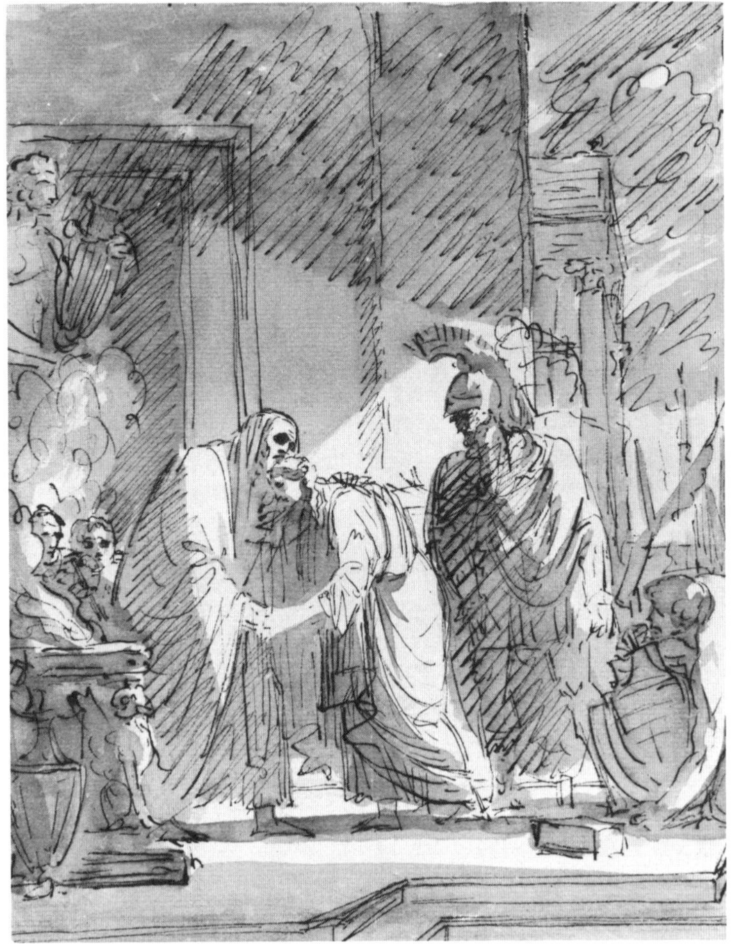

34

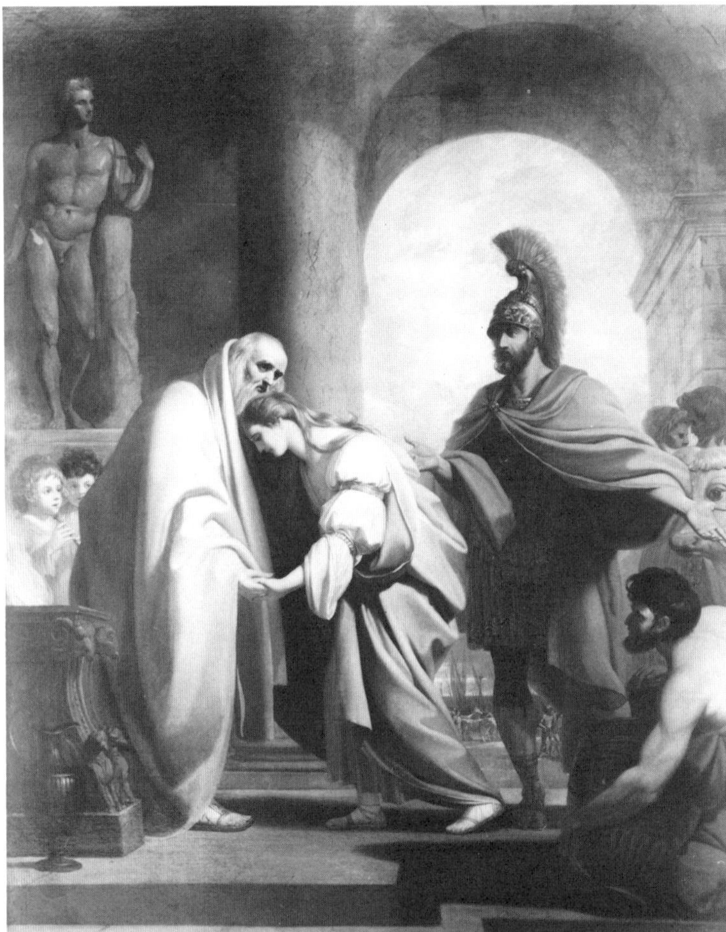

Fig. 15. *Chryseis Returned to Her Father,* 1771. New York Historical Society, New York, New York.

three times; however, only one is known today, and it bears little resemblance to the Historical Society's drawing. The extant painting, now in a private collection, follows the norm by depicting Cymon admiring Iphigenia as she sleeps. For the drawing, however, West chose the moment Iphigenia awakes to see Cymon standing over her.

The date on the drawing, 1788, does not correspond with any of the three paintings by West of this subject. However, another Historical Society drawing depicting a similar pastoral love scene, *Rinaldo and Armida* (cat. 32), is also dated 1788. From their similarity in subject, their use of drapery as a framing device, and their inclusion of amoretti, these two drawings appear to be sketches for two companion paintings, which were never executed.

MYTHOLOGY AND ALLEGORY

34 *Chryseis Returned to Her Father*

c. 1771 or 1777

ink and sepia

8¾ x 6¾

Inscribed on reverse: Chryseis Restored to Her Father

Benj West

The scene of Odysseus returning Chryseis to her father Chryses, the priest of Apollo, is from Homer's *Iliad* (Book I). The reunion takes place at the entrance to the temple of Apollo. In the left foreground of the drawing is the altar to Apollo, on which a sacrificial fire burns. In the background stands a statue of the god holding a lyre. Beside Odysseus, one of his men presents an offering to appease Apollo. In the distance are the masts of the Greek ships.

All the elements of the story are also present in West's painting of the same subject, now in the New York Historical Society (fig. 15). The painting recreates the general composition and the position of the major figures in the drawing. The one significant difference is the introduction of the arch that frames Odysseus and isolates him from Chryseis and her father. West used the arch as a common element in the companion painting of *Aeneas and Creusa*, also in the New York Historical Society collection.[37] The Historical Society's drawing does have a companion drawing, but it depicts *The Continence of Scipio* (see cat. 22), not *Aeneas and Creusa*.

The painting of *Chryseis Returned to Her Father* is signed and dated, but the date is unclear and is variously read as 1771 and 1777. A sketch of the same subject with a very different composition is in the collection of the Pierpont Morgan Library. As Ruth Kraemer notes, the Morgan Library sketch perhaps is West's first visualization of the subject, while the Historical Society drawing exhibits a more developed idea, very close to the finished painting.[38]

35 *Adonis Departing for the Hunt*

ink wash and white chalk

8½ x 6¼

Adonis was the offspring of an incestuous relationship between Cinyras, the King of Cyprus, and his daughter Myrrha. Out of shame, Myrrha asked the gods to punish her. She was turned into a myrrh tree and Adonis was born from the trunk of the tree. The infant was raised by Venus, the goddess of love. Her motherly love for Adonis grew into passion as he grew into an attractive young man. Venus' lover, Apollo, became jealous of Adonis and sent a wild boar that mortally gored the youth while he was hunting.

West's drawing depicts Adonis as he departs for the hunt with his spear in his right hand, his four dogs on the leash in his left hand, and his game bag over his shoulder. He turns to his left to look at someone outside the picture plane. The hand on the right edge of the paper near his leg probably belongs to Venus, who, out of concern for his safety, begs him not to go. Apparently, the composition was continued on a second sheet. The drawing is not dated and no painting of this subject by West is known.

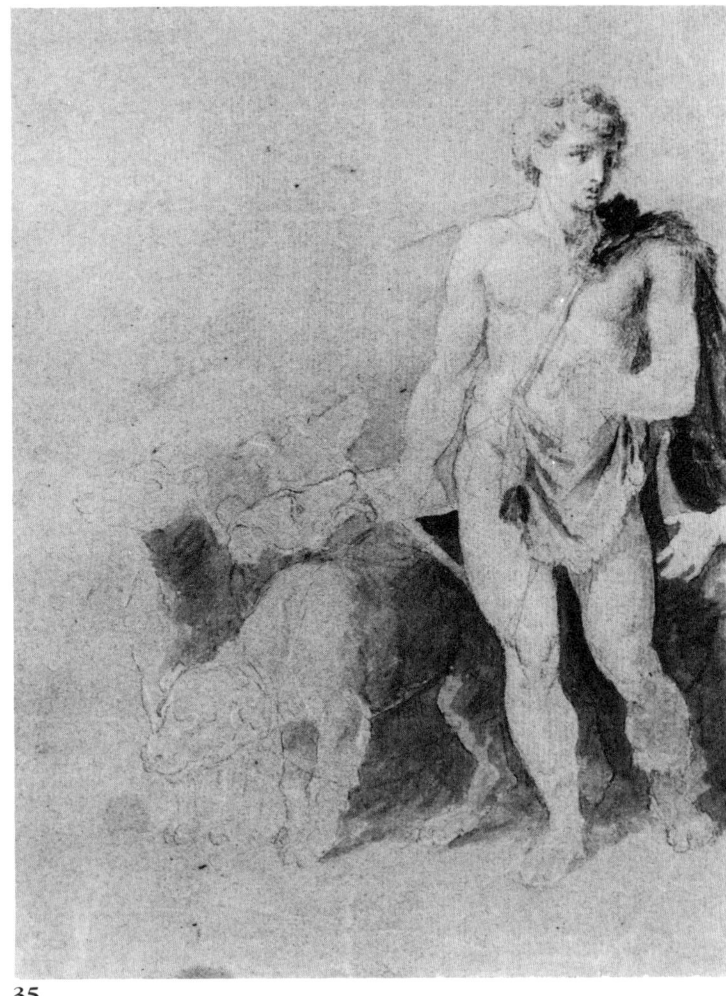
35

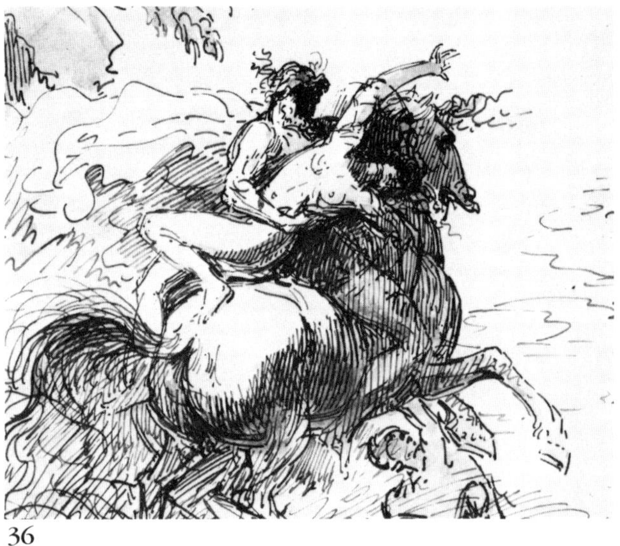
36

36 *The Rape of Persephone*

ink, sepia wash, and blue wash

6 x 7

Signed: BW

Inscribed on reverse: Rape of Persephone Benj West

According to Ovid's *Metamorphosis* (5:385–424) and *Fasti* (4:417–450), Persephone was abducted by Pluto, the king of the underworld, and carried back to his subterranean kingdom in his chariot. West's choice to depict Pluto on horseback was probably an aesthetic decision based on composition design. The concentrated power of the intertwining figures of Pluto, Persephone, and the horse in this drawing would be lost with the introduction of a chariot. West uses his hatching drawing style at its heaviest here to convey the energy and dynamics of the scene.

The drawing is not dated and is not related to any of West's known paintings.

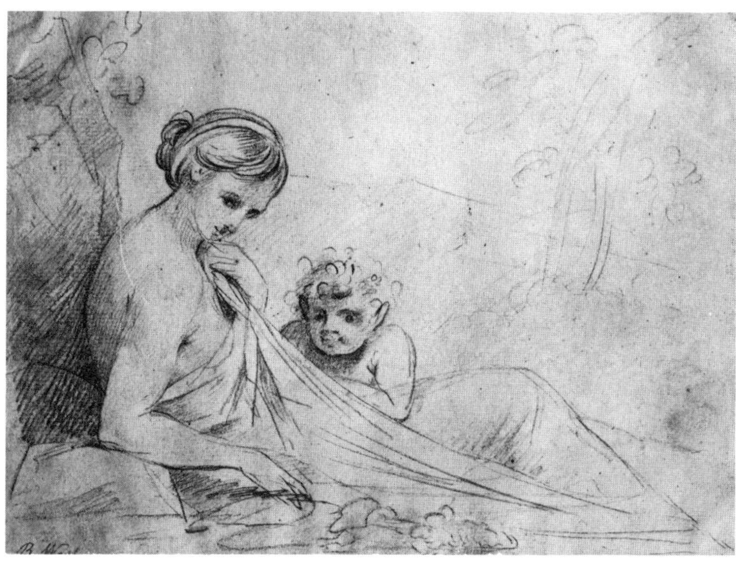

37

37 *A Nymph and Satyr*

graphite

5¾ x 7⅜

Signed: B. West

Inscribed on reverse: Benj West

In Greek mythology, nymphs and satyrs were divinities of nature. The daughters of Zeus and the sky, nymphs were born out of rain and springs, and were attributed with fertilizing and nourishing powers. Nymphs are depicted as beautiful young women enjoying nature, usually nude or half-clothed. Satyrs represent the uncontrollable forces of plant and animal life. They appear as men with curly hair, animal ears, hoofed feet, and usually with horns on their head.

The drawing depicts a nymph seated in a pastoral setting, with a young satyr leaning on her leg. She pulls at her garment to cover herself as she and her companion look outward to engage the viewer. The drawing is not dated, and this composition does not relate to any of West's known paintings.

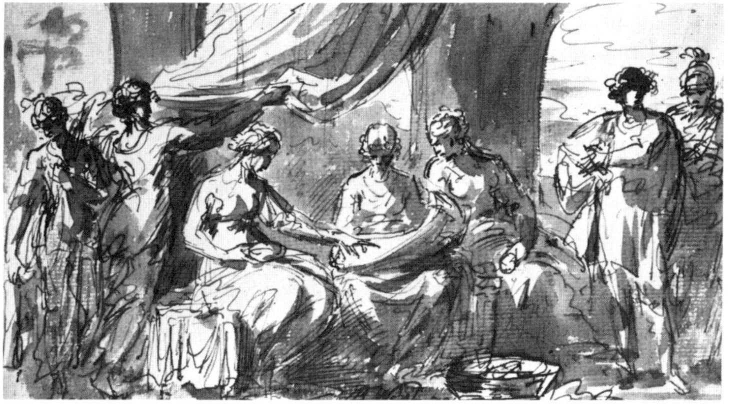

38

38 *Classical Subject*

1784

sepia and wash

5⅜ x 9½

Signed: B West 1784

The subject of this drawing is unidentified. It depicts three seated female figures, perhaps sibyls or goddesses, studying an object, a scroll or cradle, held by the center figure. The two flanking women appear to hold smaller objects. To the right of the three central figures stand two males, perhaps messengers. One wears a helmet, and the other appears to wear a laurel crown. Behind, and to the left of the women are two female servants, one of which pulls aside drapery revealing the arcade in the background.

Aside from the unidentified subject, another curious aspect of this drawing is the resemblance the three central figures bear to the three goddesses from the east pediment of the Parthenon (fig. 16).

These figures were among those brought to England by Thomas Bruce, the Earl of Elgin. West is known to have studied the marbles for three months during the winter of 1807–08. Furthermore, West admitted to incorporating the classical figures into his own compositions. In February 1808 he wrote to Lord Elgin:

> In order to render the subject which I selected, with perspicuity. . . . I have ventured to unite figures of my own invention with those of Phidias . . . . by arranging his figures in my own compositions, and adapting them to subjects, by which my sketches may be rendered more acceptable, as well as more improving to myself in the higher point of my profession.[39]

However, since the drawing is dated 1784, thirty-seven years before the first of the Elgin Marbles arrived in England and forty-three years before Lord Elgin made them available to West, any resemblance to the Parthenon goddesses cannot be the result of West's direct knowledge of the sculptures. The first published images of the Parthenon sculptures appeared in Stuart and Revett's *Antiquities of Athens* in 1787, still three years after West's drawing, however, the engravings were done after Stuart's drawings, some executed as early as the 1750s.[40] West could have seen Stuart's drawings prior to 1784.

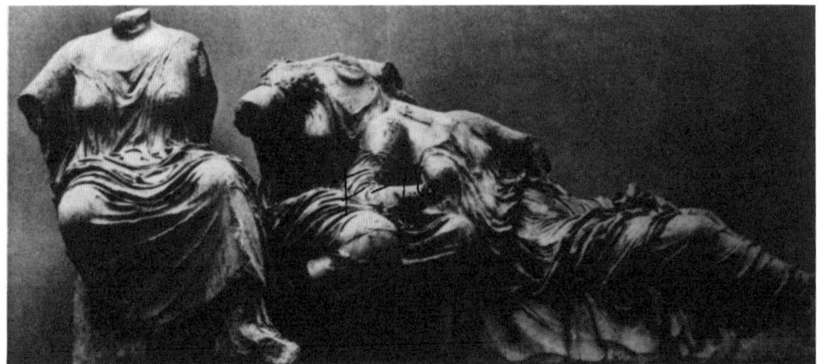

Fig. 16. *Three Goddesses,* from the east pediment of the Parthenon. British Museum, London, England.

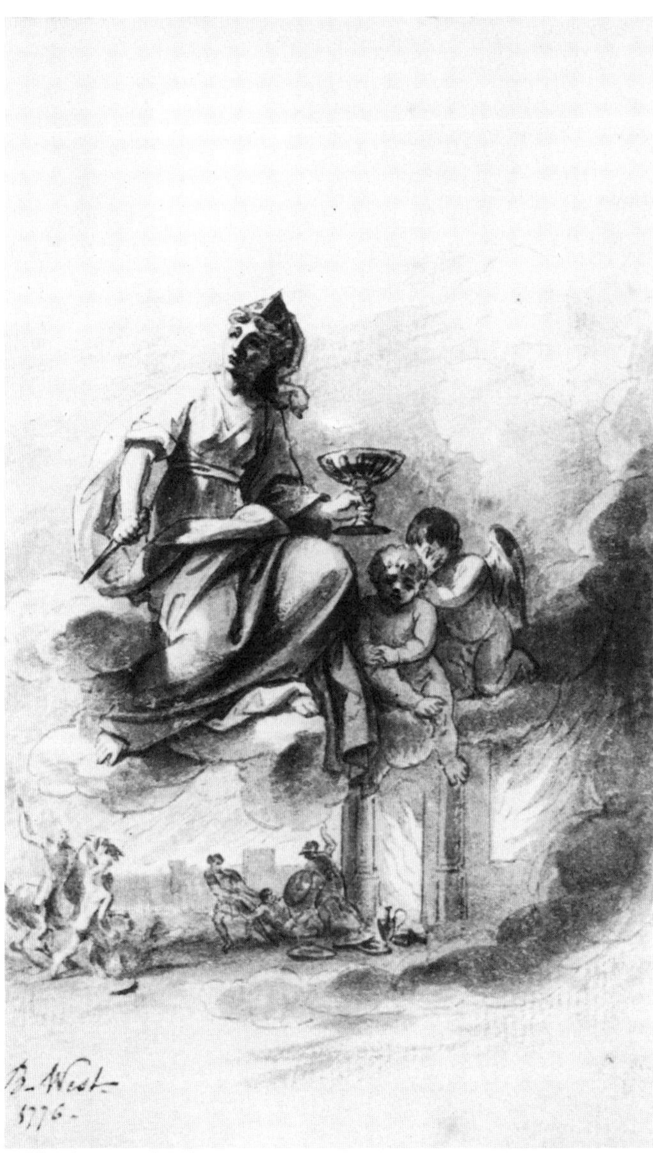

39 *The Tragic Muse*

1776

ink and sepia wash

6 x 3½

Signed: B. West 1776

Inscribed on reverse: The Tragic Muse Benj West

Melpomene, the muse of tragedy, is usually identifiable by her familiar tragic mask, a horn or a crown held in her hand. Beginning in the seventeenth century, a dagger or sword became a common attribute. West's tragic muse clutches a dagger in one hand and a chalice in the other. She wears a crown on her head and a look of despair on her face. Two weeping putti float with her on a cloud of smoke billowing from a flaming embattled city below. This composition was copied in every detail by engraver Francesco Bartolozzi[41] and reproduced on the title page of Volume X of the *New English Theatre,* a set of twelve volumes published in 1776 and 1777 containing the most successful plays presented in London theatres.

40 *The Tragic Muse*

c. 1776

ink

4¾ x 6⅝

Signed: B. W.

Inscribed on reverse: Benj West

This drawing includes many of the same attributes — the dagger, chalice and crown — that appear in the previous drawing. Both Muses float on clouds, and their poses are nearly identical. These similarities suggest that this undated line drawing might have been a preliminary sketch for the more finished version dated 1776. Of the two, however, this quick sketch is fresher and more dynamic. The muscular features of this Muse make her appear more aggressive. The expression on her face is more one of anger than the sorrow expressed by the Muse in the previous drawing.

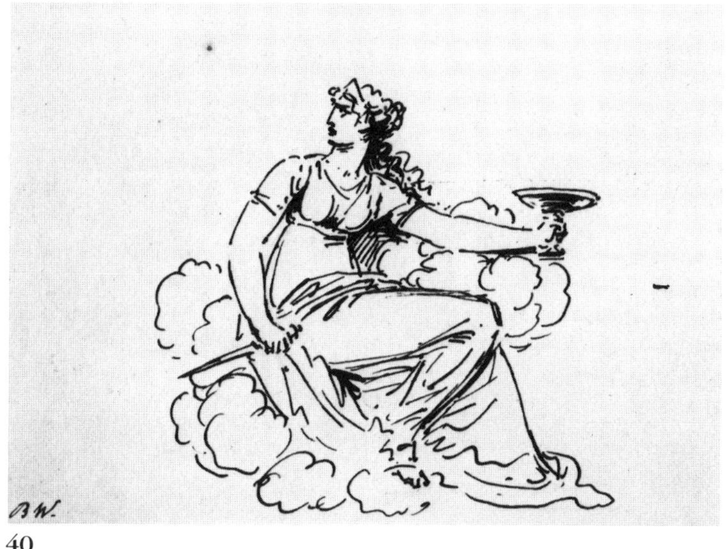

40

Notes

[1]Other sketches in the sketchbook bear resemblance to paintings done by West during his American period. These similarities have been noted by William Sawitzky in "The American Work of Benjamin West," *The Pennsylvania Magazine of History and Biography,* vol. LXII, no. 4, October 1938, pp. 433–62.

[2]Robert Alberts, *Benjamin West: A Biography* (Boston: Houghton Mifflin Company, 1978), p. 18.

[3]George Everett Hastings, *The Life and Work of Francis Hopkinson* (Chicago: University of Chicago Press, 1926).

[4]Alberts, pp. 23, 66–67, 75.

[5]Helmut von Erffa and Allen Staley, *The Paintings of Benjamin West* (New Haven and London: Yale University Press, 1986), p. 156, note 47.

[6]Ibid., p. 38 and 156, note 47.

[7]Joseph Farington, *The Diary of Joseph Farington,* vol. X, July 1809–December 1810, edited by Kathryn Care (New Haven and London: Yale University Press, 1982), p. 3627.

[8]Ibid., p. 3675.

[9]Thomas G. Morton and Frank Woodbury, *The History of the Pennsylvania Hospital 1751–1895* (Philadelphia, 1895), p. 309.

[10]Erffa and Staley, p. 374.

[11]Ibid., p. 363.

[12]Ibid.

[13]Ibid., p. 365.

[14]Ibid.

[15]Ibid., p. 384.

[16]Ibid., p. 578.

[17]Ibid., pp. 384–86.

[18]Ibid.

[19]Ibid., p. 173.

[20]Ibid., p. 256.

[21]Tacitus, *Annals,* I, 58, translated by Alfred John Church and William Jackson Brodribb (New York, 1942), p. 21.

[22]Erffa and Staley, p. 178.

[23]Ruth S. Kraemer, *Drawings by Benjamin West and His Son Raphael Lamar West* (New York: The Pierpont Morgan Library, 1975), p. 19.

[24]Tacitus, p. 39.

[25]Erffa and Staley, p. 178.

[26]Ibid. 164, 179.

[27]Tacitus, p. 79.

[28]Erffa and Staley, p. 181.

[29]Ibid., p. 182.

[30]Ibid., pp. 182–83.

[31]Ibid., p. 183.

[32]E. B. Fryde, *The Great Revolt of 1381* (London: The Historical Association, 1981), p. 24.

[33]Hume, *History of England,* introduction to *Wat Tyler: A Dramatic Poem* by Robert Southey (London: Sherwood, Neeley, and Jones, 1817), p. X.

[34]Robert Southey, *Wat Tyler: A Dramatic Poem* (London: Sherwood, Neeley, and Jones, 1817).

[35]Geoffrey Carnell, *Robert Southey and His Age. The Development of Conservative Mind* (Oxford: Clavendon Press, 1960), pp. 162–63.

[36]Alberts, p. 349.

[37]Erffa and Staley, p. 256.

[38]Kraemer, p. 12.

[39]Erffa and Staley, p. 439.

[40]James Stuart and Nicholas Revett, *Antiquities of Athens* (London, 1789).

[41]A. Calabi, *Francesco Bartolozzi, Catalogue des Estampes* (Milan, 1928), cited in Kraemer, p. 10.

Other Drawings by West in the Historical Society's Collection

GENRE

Ox

1787
ink
8½ x 13¼
Signed: B. West
Inscribed on front: The ox brought from Lord Warwick's Park and shown to His Majesty at Windsor
Jany 1st 1787

Woman Sewing

ink
5⅛ x 4⅜
Signed: B. W.
Inscribed on reverse: Benj West

Figure Studies

graphite and sepia
10¼ x 6

Street Scene with Cripple

sepia with wash
4¾ x 7½
Inscribed on reverse: Benj West

Group of People

sepia with wash
6¼ x 8⅞
Inscribed on reverse: Benj West

Seated Man

graphite
5¼ x 3¾
Signed: B. W.
Inscribed on reverse: Benj West

Angels Announcing the Birth of Christ

ink and wash

8½ x 7¼ oval

Inscribed on reverse: Angels Announcing the Birth of Our Saviour, Sketch for the picture in the Cathedral at Rochester. Benj West

Christ Disputing with the Doctors

(fig. 17)

ink

11 x 7⅜

Inscribed on reverse: Study for the figure of Christ disputing with the Doctors. Benj West

Christ in the Wilderness

1810

ink

12⅝ x 8¾

Signed: B. West 1810

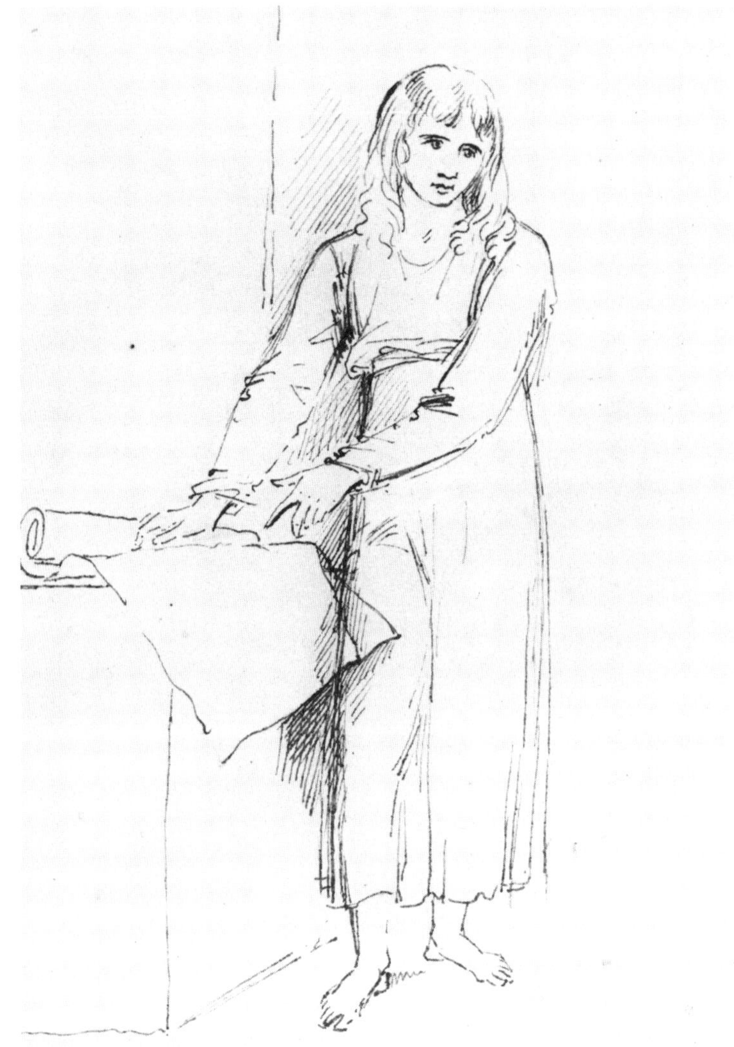

Fig. 17. *Christ Disputing with the Doctors*

LITERATURE

The Captive

graphite and sepia wash

6⅛ x 5

Inscribed on front: Barabus

Inscribed on reverse: The Captive, a study for the Picture Benj West

MYTHOLOGICAL

A Nest of Cupids

graphite

4½ x 6⅛

Signed: B. W.

Inscribed on reverse: A Nest of Cupids. Benj West

Hector Parting with His Wife

sepia and chalk on blue paper

12¾ x 9

Inscribed on reverse: Hector parting with his wife and child at Scoean Gate. A sketch for the picture painted for Dr. Newton, Bishop of Bristol

Sketchbook Drawings

(Each sheet is 6½ x 3⅞ inches)

folio

1 *Full-length Male Figure with Hat in Hand*

graphite

1a *Architectural Sketch*

graphite

inscribed in ink: Robert Enoch Hobart 1779

5th April 1820 R. E. Hobart

2 *Three-quarter-length Male Figure*

graphite

2a *Six Heads*

graphite and ink

3 *Three-quarter-length Male Figure with Hat Under Arm*

graphite

3a *Two Half-length Female Figures*

graphite

4 *Full-length Seated Female Figure with Child*

graphite

4a *Three-quarter-length Male Figure with Hat Under Arm*

graphite and ink

5 *Three-quarter-length Female Figure*

graphite

5a *Detail Study of Female Hand Holding a Flower*

graphite

6 *Three-quarter-length Male Figure with Drapery over Arm*

graphite

6a *Three-quarter-length Female Figure with Arms Crossed*

graphite

7 *Three-quarter-length Female Figure with Arms Crossed*

graphite

7a *Three-quarter-length Male Figure (vertical) and Three-quarter-length Female Figure (horizontal)*

graphite

8 *Full-length Helmeted Nude Figure with Child*

graphite

8a *Full-length Female Figure with Garland of Flowers*

graphite

9 *Full-length Female Figure*

graphite

9a *Male Figure Bowing to Female Figure*

graphite

10 *Male Leaning on the Back of a Chair, Female Figure Seated in Chair*

(cat. 2)
graphite
identified as Francis Hopkinson

10a *Half-length Male Figure (vertical) and Half-length Female Figure (horizontal)*

graphite

11 *Two Female Figures and Four Male Figures Playing Cards*

graphite

11a *Three-quarter-length Male Figure and Half-length Male Figure in Oval*

graphite

12 *Three-quarter-length Male Figure, Half-length Male Figure in Oval and Three-quarter-length Male Figure*

graphite

12a *Three-quarter-length Male Figure in Square and Half-length Female Figure in Oval*

graphite

13 *Three-quarter-length Male Figure and Half-length Female Figure*

graphite

13a *Half-length Male Figure*

graphite
identified as John Green (painter)

14 *Three-quarter-length Male Figure*

graphite

14a *Three-quarter-length Male Figure*

graphite

15 *Three-quarter-length Male Figure with Hat in Hand with Detail Study on Head*

graphite

15a *Three-quarter-length Male Figure*
graphite

16 *Three-quarter-length Female Figure*
graphite

16a *Half-length Female Figure in Oval*
graphite

17 *Three-quarter-length Female Figure*
graphite

17a *Three-quarter-length Male Figure Seated With Young Female Figure*
graphite

18 *Full-length Winged Figure Wearing a Helmet*
graphite

18a *Three-quarter-length Male Figure Seated*
graphite
identified as John West (father of Benjamin)

19 *Half-length Male Figure*
graphite

20 *Half-length Female Figure (vertical)*
ink
identified by Sawitzky as Mary Inglis

Full-length Female Figure Seated (horizontal)
graphite and ink

20a *Full-length Winged Figure Wearing a Helmet*
graphite

21 *Three-quarter-length Female Figure*
graphite and ink

21a *Three-quarter-length Female Figure*
graphite and ink

22 *Two Full-length Male Figures Fighting*
graphite

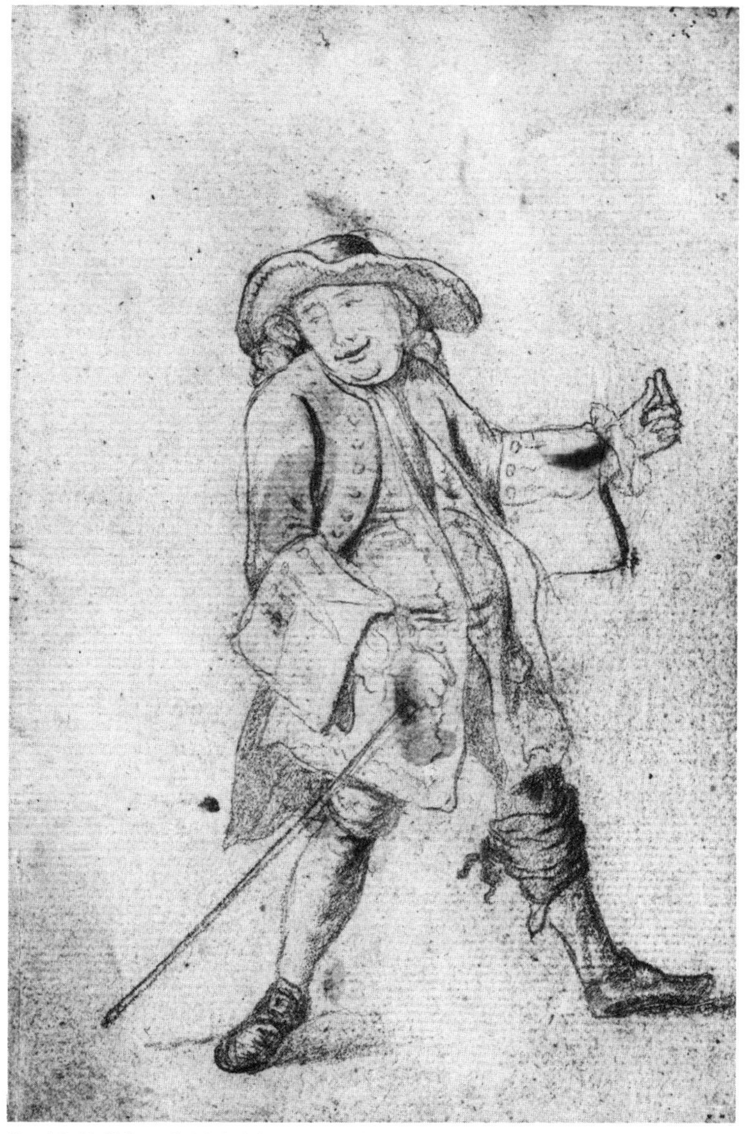

Fig. 18. *Full-length Male Figure Laughing.*

22a *Three-quarter-length Female Figure with Garland*

graphite

identified by Sawitzky as Jane Galloway

23 *Mercury*

graphite

23a *Full-length Male Figure Walking with Cane*

graphite

identified as David James Dove (schoolmaster)

24 *Full-length Male Figure Laughing*

(fig. 18)

graphite

24a *Full-length Male Figure Walking*

graphite

identified as Shewel, brother of Stephen

25 *Full-length Male Figure Jumping on Hat in Anger*

graphite with ink scribbles

identified as Thomson, a barber

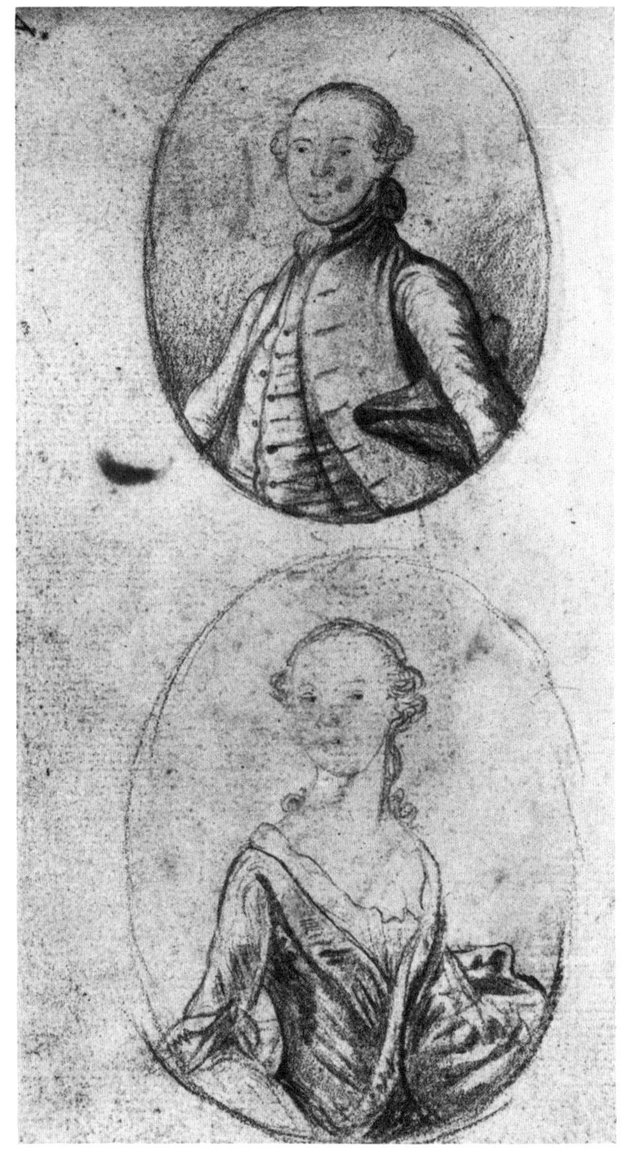

Fig. 19. *Self-Portrait in Oval.*

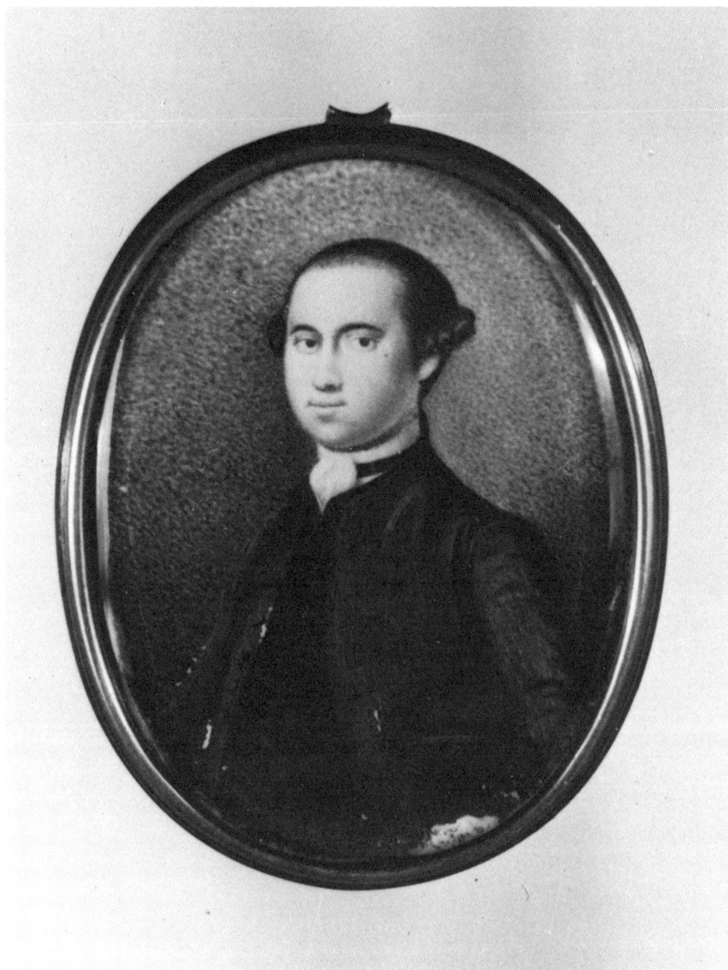

Fig. 20. *Self-Portrait,* c.1758–59. Yale University Art Gallery, New Haven, Connecticut. The Lelia A. and John Hill Morgan Collection.

25a *Half-length Self-Portrait in Oval and Half-length Female Figure in Oval*

(fig. 19)

graphite

26 *Three-quarter-length Female Figure Seated with Flower in Hand*

(cat. 1)

graphite

identified by Sawitzky as Mrs. George Ross

26a *Full-length Male Figure Walking with Stick under Arm*

graphite

identified as Sammy Worral

27 *Full-length Figure of Dead Christ*

ink

Angel

graphite

27a *Half-length Female Figure*

graphite

28 *Full-length Female Figure Seated and Detail Study of Hand*

graphite

28a *Three-quarter-length Male Figure*

graphite

MUSEUM OF ART STAFF

JAMES MOESER
Dean, College of Arts and Architecture, and Director, University Arts Services

SANFORD SIVITZ SHAMAN
Director

WILLIAM HULL
Director Emeritus

OLGA K. PREISNER
Curator

CHARLES GAROIAN
Education Director

RANDY PLOOG
Assistant Curator

OK HI LEE
Registrar

RONALD HAND
Exhibition Designer

LUCINDA SALATINO
Museum Store Manager

BARBARA WEAVER
Secretary to the Director

BETSY WARNER
Secretary

ROBERT E. FRY
Chief of Security

All photographs of the Historical Society drawings were taken by Louis Meehan.

Catalog Design: Marilyn Shoboken

Produced by the Penn State Department of Publications U.Ed. 87-761